WESLEY
GOLD

WESLEY
GOLD

COMPILED BY RAY COMFORT

Bridge-Logos
Orlando, Florida 32822

Bridge-Logos

Orlando, FL 32822 USA

Wesley Gold
by Ray Comfort

Copyright ©2007 by Bridge-Logos

Printed in the United States of America.

Library of Congress Catalog Card Number: 2007930144
International Standard Book Number 978-0-88270-408-1

Unless otherwise indicated, Scripture quotations are from the *Holy Bible: King James Version.*

G163.315.N.m706.35250

My sincere thanks to
Giancarlo Jarquin and Trisha Ramos
for their editorial research.

Table of Contents

Foreword ix

Biography of John Wesley 1

Illustration Portfolio 35

Wesley Gold 47

Note: Much of the information in this book is taken directly from John Wesley's Journal.[1]

---

1 *The Journal of John Wesley,* John Wesley (Appreciation of the Journal by Augustine Birrell, K.C., Moody Press (Chicago). ISBN: 0-8024-4390-7. Edited by Percy Livingstone Parker

Foreword

*W*esley Gold cracks open the rock of the historical record and exposes precious and shimmering nuggets that the contemporary Church needs in its hands. Wesley was an open air preacher. His famous "The world is my parish," was nothing more than an echo of his Master's heart.

I loved compiling *Spurgeon Gold*. The Prince of Preachers spoke precious nuggets, even in his sleep. I also enjoyed *Whitefield Gold*. I felt as though I got to know someone whom I had only previously known from a distance.

But there is something different that excited me about John Wesley. I can identify with him because he was an open air preacher, rather than an indoor pulpit expositor. He knew the effectiveness of reaching sinners the way Jesus did. There is nothing like a good open air, with angry hecklers ... and listening sinners.

John Wesley knew the heartbeat of God. He understood the reason for the cross. It was to save sinners from a fiery and terrifying Hell, and he busied his life in warning them. He preached like there was no tomorrow for himself or for his hearers.

He would no doubt be bared from modern pulpits. He wasn't a motivational speaker. He wasn't seeker-friendly. He called Hell what it is. He preached sin, righteousness and judgment. He didn't compromise the message because he feared only God.

John Wesley was a normal biblical Christian, and if he stands out from you and I, that's to our shame. We should (like the Apostles in the Book of Acts, and John Wesley) be consumed with the Great Commission. Little else should matter compared to it. This is the spirit of Paul's admonition:

"But this I say, brethren, the time is short: it remains, that both they that have wives be as though they had none; and they that weep, as though they wept not; and they that rejoice, as though they rejoiced not; and they that buy, as though they possessed not; and they that use this world, as not abusing it: for the fashion of this world passes away" (1 Corinthians 7:29–31).

John Wesley said, "When you're on fire for God, people will show up just to watch you burn." It is my prayer that this book will get you on fire for God.

Ray Comfort

John Wesley

1703–1791

Evangelist and
Founder of Methodism

John Wesley was an Anglican clergyman, evangelist, and cofounder of Methodism, which evolved into the Methodist Church. He was born on June 17, 1703, in a rectory in Epworth, a small town and civil parish on the Isle of Axholme, North Lincolnshire, England—now famous for being the birthplace of John and Charles Wesley. John was the fifteenth of nineteen children born to Samuel and Susanna Wesley. His full name when he was christened appears to have been John Benjamin, but he never used the middle name or initial. Charles Wesley, his equally famous brother and cofounder of Methodism, was born on December 18, 1707. Nine of Samuel and Susanna's children died as infants. Four of the children that died were twins. A maid accidentally smothered one child. When Susanna died, only eight of her children were still alive.

John Wesley's father, Samuel Wesley (1662–1735), was the son and grandson of clergy; he was orphaned when a child. When a young man, he attended Newington Green, a private school for dissenters, in preparation for becoming a clergy in that movement. There he met Daniel Defoe, who was also a student, and who would later write the novels Robinson Crusoe and Moll Flanders. Originally Samuel was a Nonconformist, but converted to the Church of England while at Oxford. He served the parish of Epworth in North Lincolnshire for almost forty years. Although now known as the father of a great religious leader, in his own time Samuel was known by many as a poet and a writer of controversial prose. He was also known for his strictness with his parishioners, which angered many of them.

John Wesley's mother, Susanna Wesley (1669–1742), was a remarkable woman in wisdom and intelligence. She was born in 1669, the youngest of twenty-five children in the family of Dr. Samuel Annesley, a well-known, powerful minister. Her parents were gracious and tireless workers who kept a pleasant home. Her father's study was a hub of intellectual activity where many famous men of the day debated on current issues. Susanna inherited much of her character from her father.

Once in 1711, when her husband was in London for an extended period attending a church Convocation, Susanna started the practice of reading the Bible and sermons to her family and instructing them. One of the servants told his parents and they asked if they could come. When given permission, they told others, and they came, until the immediate attendance amounted to nearly forty, which rapidly increased until there were over two hundred, and the parsonage could not contain all that came. Susanna read to them the best and most awakening sermons she could find in her husband's library, and talked to the people freely and affectionately about the things of God. When asked about the meetings, she said they were held because "the end of the institution of the Sabbath was not fully answered by attending church unless the intermediate spaces of time were filled up by other acts of devotion."

The curate of their church, a man named Inman, became jealous because more were attending her meetings than his, so he wrote to Mr. Wesley complaining about them, saying that they would scandalize the church and that they should not be tolerated any longer. When her husband wrote to her that she should get someone else to read the sermons, Susanna replied to him that there was not a man who could read a sermon without spoiling it.

The curate continued to complain to the Rector, and he wrote to his wife again telling her that the meetings should be discontinued. Susanna wrote back detailing how good the meetings were doing and telling him that none were opposed to the meetings except Mr. Inman and one other person. She finished her letter by saying, "If after all this you think fit to dissolve this assembly do not tell me you desire me to do it, for that will not satisfy my conscience; but send your positive command in such full and express terms as may absolve me from all guilt and punishment for neglecting this opportunity for doing good when you and I shall appear before the great and awful tribunal of our Lord Jesus Christ." That ended the matter and nothing more was said about discontinuing her meetings.

It's no wonder Isaac Taylor wrote that "the mother of the Wesleys was the mother of Methodism;" and that, "when she said in her letter, 'Do not advise me, but command me to desist,' she was putting in place a cornerstone of the future of Methodism." Only eternity will reveal the influence that these meetings, which were always attended by the Wesley children, had on John and Charles in future years.

Susanna Wesley not only taught her children spiritual discipline but also physical discipline and restraint. For example, she trained her children to refuse food between meals, and John's characteristic and polite reply to all kindly offers was, "I thank you; I will think of it." This discipline Susanna taught her children was of great value years later when Wesley was traveling many miles on horseback to evangelistic meetings.

With regard to this kind of training, Dr. Overton, a future Rector of the church, wrote, "One pictures John Wesley at Epworth as a grave, sedate child, always wanting to know the reason of everything, one of a group of remarkable children, of whom his sister Martha was most like him in appearance and character; each of them with a strong individuality and a very high spirit, but all well kept in hand by their admirable mother, all precise and rather formal, after the manner of their day, in their language and habits."

One of Susanna's methods of teaching was what John later referred to as "memory drills," which consisted of repeating the thing to be learned over and over, often far more times than Samuel Wesley thought was necessary. Once he said quite impatiently to his wife, "Why do you go over the same thing with that child the twentieth time?"

"Because," she said, "nineteen times were not sufficient. If had stopped after telling him nineteen times, all my labor would have been lost."

In a letter to her husband in London in 1712, Susanna tells him that John, now nine, is sick and gives a glimpse of the character that was developing in him: "Jack has borne his disease bravely, like a man, and indeed like a Christian, without any complaint, though he seemed angry at the smallpox when they were sore, as we guessed by his looking sourly at them, for he never said anything."

When he was still a child his father once told him, "Child, you think to carry everything by dint [force] of argument; but you will find how very little is ever done in the world by close reason." In speaking of this years later, John commented, "Very little indeed."

The Rector was as strict with his ungodly parishioners as Susanna was with their children, but where it created character and love in her children, it created rebellion and hate in many of the parishioners who wanted to continue in their sins and not be constantly reprimanded for them and made to feel guilty. So there was a constant conflict between them and the righteous Samuel. He did his best but he did not know how to win their love without compromising his preaching.

The ungodly people, who made up most of his parishioners, would not contribute to the support of the church or the Rector and his family, so his debts increased until he could no longer pay them. That meant debtor's prison.

In 1705, when John was two years old, Samuel was arrested in the churchyard for a debt of £30 and taken off to prison in Lincoln Castle. Susanna sent him her rings to sell, but he returned them, believing the Lord would provide otherwise. Taking advantage of his prison time, the good Rector spread the gospel among his "fellow jailbirds" by reading prayers and preaching. He even secured some religious books to distribute among the prisoners.

He wrote to his wife, "I am now at rest. I am come to the haven where I've long expected to be." And at another time he wrote, "A jail is a paradise in comparison of the life I led before I came hither. No man has worked truer for bread than I have done, and few have lived harder, or their families either."

When he was released from prison and returned home, his rest ended as his battles with the ungodly in his parish picked up again. Finally some of them decided that the only way to rid themselves of their tormentor was to burn down the rectory, which was a typical country parsonage of the seventeenth century, a homely, two-story, frame structure, plastered within and roofed with straw.

It was on Wednesday night, February 9, 1709. Susanna had been sick for several days and was upstairs in bed in her room. Her two oldest daughters were in the room with her, keeping her company. Bettie, their maid, and five younger children were in the nursery. Another daughter, Hettie, was alone in a small bedroom next to the granary, where threshed wheat and corn were stored. John, now six, was in his room.

At 10:30 Samuel left his study and locked the door to safeguard his manuscripts and records of his family and parish. He retired to a room near his wife. Outside a northeast storm was blowing in, and dark clouds nearly obscured the half moon. At the back of the house dark figures crept closer with unlit torches in their hands. When they reached the walls of the house they lit the torches and threw them up onto the straw roof. The dry straw caught fire immediately and, whipped by the wind, the fire raced up the roof until it was a carpet of flames.

Inside the house burning straw fell upon Hettie's bed, burning her arms. Screaming, she ran to her father's room. Outside in the street passersby had seen the flames and were yelling, "Fire! Fire!" Samuel raced through the house, wakening and warning his family and helping Susanna out of bed and down the stairs. Bettie appeared through the now dense smoke with Charles in her arms and the three children following her. Samuel helped them into the yard and over the garden wall. Then he rushed back to the house to find Susanna who had become separated from him. But he could not find her anywhere. He also tried to get to his study but it was impossible because of the smoke and flames.

Then he heard what no parent wants to hear, the voice of one of his children crying, "Help me!" from within the house. It was John—he had awakened to find the ceiling of his room on fire and falling down upon him. His distraught father tried to force his way up the stairs to John's room, but sheets of flame forced him back. He and the other children committed John's soul to God.

On the bottom floor of the house, Susanna tried to find the opened front door, but was driven back by a blinding wall of flame and smoke. Twice she tried without success. On a third attempt she was literally blown down to the floor by the violence of the fire and wind. Calming herself, she asked for divine help. Then she saw an unburned cloak and wrapped it about her chest and waded knee-deep through the flames to the door. Her legs were scorched, and her face was so black with smoke that when her frantic husband found her he did not recognize her.

Upstairs, six-year-old John climbed onto a chest near the window, and cried for someone to help him. Two men raced to the window. One stood upon the shoulders of the other and John leaped into his arms. At that moment, almost as if it had been previously held back, the flaming roof fell into the room, devouring everything in it in flames.

John was carried to his mother and she took him into her arms. When Samuel found her, she was holding John, who he thought had been burned to ashes. He could hardly get himself to believe that the boy was safe, and he kissed him repeatedly until the reality of it came.

Though in pain, Susanna asked him, "Are your books safe?"

"Let them go," Samuel replied, "now that you and all the children are preserved." He called to those who were near him, "Come, neighbors, let us kneel down; let us give thanks to God. He has given me all my eight children. Let the house go; I am rich enough."

More than forty years later, this was still John Wesley's most vivid memory. He said that from that moment there was no room in his thoughts for any doubt that there was a God whose mercy interposes in moments of danger. Susanna's escape was as miraculous as that of her son's. In later years John had a vignette of a burning house engraved beneath his portrait, with these words imprinted: "Is not this a brand plucked from the burning?"

As soon as John and his two brothers were old enough to leave home, arrangements were made for them to continue their education in the best schools that England offered. Samuel, the oldest, went to Westminster School in 1704, then to Oxford University. About ten years later, around 1714, he returned to Westminster as a teacher. This was about the time John, the second oldest, was entering the Charterhouse. Charles, who was the youngest, entered Westminster School in 1716. So for a few years before John went up to Oxford, all three of Samuel's boys were in London together.

In 1738 John Wesley wrote about his early life at Epworth and his spiritual life at school: "The next six or seven years were spent at school where, outward restraints being removed, I was much more negligent than before, even of outward duties, and almost continually guilty of outward sins, which I knew to be such, though they were not scandalous in the eye of the world. However, I still read the Scriptures and said my prayers morning and evening, and what I now hoped to be saved by was: (1) not being so bad as other people; (2) having still a kindness for religion; and (3) reading the Bible, going to church, and saying my prayers."

One of his contemporaries at Christ Church, which is one of the largest colleges in the University of Oxford, described John as "the very sensible and acute collegian, baffling every man by the subtleties of logic, and laughing at them for being so easily routed; a young fellow of the finest classical taste, of the most liberal and manly sentiments;" and further said he was "gay and sprightly, with a turn for wit and humor."

John wrote sparkling letters to his friends and family. He once sent his brother Samuel several stanzas in Latin about "Cloe's Favorite Flea"; it was composed for a literary exercise. In a more serious mood he sent verses of Psalm 85 to his father, who was pleased with them, and urged him not to bury his talent under youthful frivolities. His letters to his father and mother reveal his affection for his family and his warm interest in all the little details of the home life at Epworth and at Wroote in Lincolnshire, where they moved in 1724.

It was about then that John became troubled about his health for the first time. On one occasion while he was walking in the country, his nose began to bleed violently. He stopped it by the somewhat drastic method of jumping into the cold waters of a nearby river. He read a book titled Health and Long Life, written by a man named Cheyne, who pleaded with his readers to lead a life of exercise and temperance. So John began to eat sparingly and drink more water, believing that these changes would benefit his health. He was also having a constant struggle "to make ends meet," even though nothing shows that he was careless with his money. His mother wrote to him about his lack of money. She said, "Dear Jack, be not discouraged; do your duty, keep close to your studies, and hope for better days. Perhaps, notwithstanding all, we shall pick up a few crumbs for you before the end of the year. Dear Jacky, I beseech Almighty God to bless thee." This was written just after he received his bachelor's degree in 1724. Two years later he was elected a fellow at Lincoln Oxford, which brought him some financial relief.

In 1725, when he was twenty-two, John came to a turning point in his life as he faced the question of what he should do with his future life. The prospect of becoming a minister was his most serious consideration, but he realized that he was spiritually unfit for the work of the ministry. He had not fallen into blatant sin, and he could not afford the expensive vices of some of the young aristocrats at Christ Church, even if he had desired them, which he did not. His mother's letters always carried with them the sweet aroma of the tender love and purity that permeated the Wesley family in Epworth. He never lost his strong love for his brothers and sisters; and his love of learning, which was always stimulated by his father's letters, kept him from an idle life.

But the spiritual fire that had burned high in him when he first came to Christ Church was now barely a flickering flame. Simply put, John Wesley had become the "gay collegian," a favorite of Oxford society, a sparkling wit, an all-around well-liked fellow. Although he maintained a good reputation for scholarship, according to his own account he was relatively indifferent to spiritual things. He wrote, "I had not all this while so much as a notion of inward holiness; nay, went on habitually, and for the most part very contentedly, in some one or other known sin, though with some intermission and short struggles, especially before and after the Holy Communion, which I was obliged to receive thrice a year." Late one night he had a conversation with one of the college porters. It was a conversation that left a lasting impression on the "merry student." The porter was working outside on a cold night, wearing only a light coat.

John said to him, "Go home and get another coat."

"This is the only coat I have in the world, and I thank God for it," the porter replied.

"Go home and get your supper, then."

"I have had nothing today but a drink of water, and I thank God for that."

"It is late, and you will be locked out, and then what will you have to thank God for?"

"I will thank him that I have the dry stones to lie upon."

"You thank God when you have nothing to wear, nothing to eat, and no bed to lie upon; what else do you thank him for?"

The porter replied, "I thank him that he has given me my life and being, a heart to love him, and a desire to serve him."

Wesley remembered the porter's word and tone for many days; they made him feel that there was something in religion that he had not yet found.

About this time he wrote to his parents to tell them that he was thinking of entering the ministry. His father's pen trembled as he wrote his reply: "You see, Time has taken me by the hand,

and Death is but a little way behind him. My eyes and heart are now almost all I have left, and I bless God for them." He cautioned John to wait to enter the ministry, so that he would not be "a callow [young and inexperienced] clergyman." And that he should check his motive carefully and be certain that it was not "as Eli's sons, to eat a piece of bread."

But his mother was a better judge of John's character, and noted the change in his tone of thought. Samuel came around, as he always did, to his wife's opinion. In a letter to John she wrote: "Mr. Wesley differs from me, and would engage you, I believe, in critical learning, which, though incidentally of use, is in nowise preferable to the other (practical divinity). I earnestly pray God to avert that great evil from you of engaging in trifling studies to the neglect of such as are absolutely necessary. I dare advise nothing. God Almighty direct and bless you!

"Now in good earnest resolve to make religion the business of your life, for, after all, that is the one thing that, strictly speaking, is necessary, and all things else are comparatively little to the purposes of life ... I heartily wish you would now enter upon a serious examination of yourself, that you may know whether you have a reasonable hope of salvation by Jesus Christ. If you have, the satisfaction of knowing it will abundantly reward your pains; if you have not, you will find a more reasonable occasion for tears than can be met with in a tragedy."

His father again cautioned him against entering the ministry for the motive of earning a livelihood, saying, "The principal spring and motive ...must certainly be the glory of God, and the service of the Church in the edification of our neighbor. And woe to him who with any meaner leading view [lesser principal motive] attempts so sacred a work."

Starting about that time and for long afterward, Wesley was highly influenced by some remarkable books that he never ceased holding in high esteem. They were Thomas à Kempis' *Imitation of Christ* (in Stanhope's translation, *The Christian Pattern*); Taylor's *Holy Living and Dying*; and later, Law's *Serious Call*, and *Christian Perfection*. Some time later, he included among them Madame Jeanne Guyon's *Experiencing Union with God Through Inner Prayer*.

The Christian Pattern deeply affected Wesley. It had been his father's favorite book, his "great and old companion," as he put it. Wesley wrote in his Journal: "The providence of God directing me to Kempis' Christian Pattern, I began to see that true religion was seated in the heart, and that God's law extended to all our thoughts as well as words and actions. I was, however, very angry at Kempis for being too strict, though I read him only in Dean Stanhope's translation ... Meeting likewise with a religious friend, which I never had till now, I began to alter the whole form of my conversation, and to set in earnest upon a new life. I set apart an hour or two a day for religious retirement. I communicated every week. I watched against all sin, whether in word or deed. I began to aim at and pray for inward holiness. So that now, 'doing so much and living so good a life,' I doubted not but I was a good Christian."

Jeremy Taylor's book, Holy Living and Dying, strengthened the convictions that had been awakened by Thomas à Kempis. "In reading several parts of this book," says Wesley, "I was exceedingly affected ... I resolved to dedicate all my life to God—all my thoughts and words and actions—being thoroughly conscious that there was no medium, but that every part of my life, not some only, must either be a sacrifice to God or to myself; that is, in effect, to the devil."

Another result of reading Taylor was Wesley's now famous journals. They hold a well-recognized place in the literature of the eighteenth century, but they were started because of Wesley's determination to make a more careful use of all his time, and to keep a record of how he used it.

Although he became somewhat of an ascetic during the next few years, with High Church beliefs, strong ritualistic tendencies, and a mystical bias, Wesley rejected Kempis' extreme doctrine of self-mortification and Taylor's morbid teaching of the necessity of constant and sorrowful uncertainty concerning personal salvation. In a letter to his mother he wrote: "If we dwell in Christ and He in us (which He will not do unless we are regenerate), certainly we must be sensible of it. If we can never have any certainty of our being in a state of salvation, good reason it is that every moment should be spent not in joy, but in fear and trembling; and then undoubtedly we are in this life of all men most miserable. God deliver us from such a fearful doctrine as this!"

Wesley first read William Law's Christian Perfection and Serious Call about 1728. Although in later years he diverged widely from Law, he never lost his admiration for the Serious Call. A short time before his death he spoke of it as a "treatise which will hardly ever be excelled, if it be equaled, in the English tongue, either for beauty of expression or for justice and depth of thought." He said that Law's two books had sowed the seed of Methodism.

In the summer of 1725, while he was preparing for his ordination, Wesley won his first convert. He told his mother how it happened: "I stole out of company at eight in the evening with a young gentleman whom I well know. As we took a turn in an aisle of St. Mary's Church, in expectation of a young lady's funeral, with whom we were both acquainted, I asked him if he really thought himself my friend; and, if he did, why he would not do me all the good he could. He began to protest, in which I cut him short by desiring him to oblige me in an instance which he could not deny to be in his own power, to let me have the pleasure of making him a whole Christian, to which I knew he was at least half persuaded already; that he could not do me a greater kindness, as both of us would be fully convinced when we came to follow that young woman." His words struck the heart of his friend and he was converted that same evening. Eighteen months later he died of consumption and Wesley preached his funeral sermon.

John's growing spiritual earnestness soon brought scorn and laughter from the college wits, and this brought a spiritual horn blast from his father: "Does anyone think the devil is dead, or asleep, or has no agents left? Surely virtue can bear being laughed at. The Captain and Master endured something more for us before he entered into glory, and unless we track his steps, in vain do we hope to share that glory with him." John and Charles Wesley owed much of their moral fiber and spiritual muscle to their father, and he shows up in many of the songs written by Charles.

On Sunday, September 19, 1725, John Wesley was ordained deacon by John Potter, Bishop of Oxford, in Christ Church Cathedral, Oxford; and ordained a priest on September 22, 1728. His first sermon was preached at South Leigh, in Oxfordshire, in 1725. Of the effectiveness of this early preaching he wrote long afterward: "Preaching was defective and fruitless, for from 1725 to 1729 I neither laid the foundation of repentance nor of preaching the Gospel, taking it for granted that all to whom I preached were believers, and that many of them needed no repentance. From 1729 to 1734, laying a deeper foundation of repentance, I saw a little fruit.

But it was only a little—and no wonder; for I did not preach faith in the blood of the covenant."

John's father was now sixty-five years old and in poor health. To continue to earn the small living from Wroote and Epworth he needed a curate—a Rector's assistant. John had been offered a school in Yorkshire; he would be the head master and only teacher. It paid a good salary, and it was secluded; both things attracted him. But his mother saw that God had better things for him in the future, and taking her advice as always, he turned down the offer. Instead, he went to Lincolnshire and worked as his father's curate for two and a quarter years, occasionally returning to Oxford. This was the only experience he ever had in pastoring a church.

On March 17, 1726, John Wesley was elected a fellow of Lincoln College. Not long afterward, in 1727, Charles Wesley entered Christ Church. Someone said that Charles was then "a bright, rollicking, young fellow 'with more genius than grace.'" When John spoke to Charles about religion he said, "What, would you have me to be a saint all at once?" and would hear no more. The rebuff did not, however, cause ill will between the brothers, and soon after John went to Wroote, Charles wrote to him with a very changed attitude, looking for the very counsel he had rejected.

Regretting his former negative response, he said, "There is no one person I would so willingly have to be the instrument of good to me as you. It is owing, in great measure, to somebody's prayers (my mother's most likely) that I am come to think as I do; for I cannot tell myself how or why I awoke out of my lethargy, only that it was not long after you went away." Almost immediately he became enthusiastic about his studies, started attending the weekly church service, and talked to others about gathering with him and seeking true holiness. Several did, and they adopted certain rules for right living, and divided their time into exact hours for study and for religious duties. They allotted as little time as possible to sleeping and eating, and as much as possible to holy devotions. They fasted until 3 p.m. on Wednesdays and Fridays, received Holy Communion once each week, studied and discussed the Greek New Testament and the Classics each evening in a member's room, and methodically brought all their lives under strict examination by each other. Because of this, it wasn't long before they were being called The Holy Club by other students to mock their emphasis on devotions and righteous living. The precision with which they regulated their lives caused one young man to say, "A new set of Methodists have sprung up."

Charles Wesley says that the name of Methodist "was bestowed upon himself and his friends because of their strict conformity to the method of study prescribed by the university." In an address to George II, John Wesley referred to his societies as "the people in derision called Methodists," and in his English Dictionary defines a Methodist as "one that lives according to the method laid down in the Bible."

Dr. Overton, a later Rector at Epworth and an Oxford graduate, said of his college peers, "A Lincoln man may be pardoned for remarking with satisfaction that Lincoln had nothing to do with the feeble jokes which were made upon these good earnest youths. Christ Church and Merton must divide the honor between them. The Holy Club, Bible Bigots, Bible Moths, Sacramentarians, Supererogation Men, Methodists—all these titles were invented by the fertile brains of 'the wits' to cast opprobrium, as they thought; but really to confer honor upon a perfectly inoffensive band of young men who only desired to be what they and their opponents were alike called—Christians. An Oxford man may, indeed, blush for his university when he reflects that these young men could not even attend the highest service of the Church without running the gauntlet of a jeering rabble, principally composed of men who were actually being prepared for the sacred ministry of that Church."

After John returned to Oxford University in 1729, he became leader of the Holy Club. He was nicknamed "the Curator of the Holy Club," or, sometimes, "the Father of the Holy Club." The old rector of Epworth, hearing of John's new title, wrote: "If this be so, I am sure I am the grandfather of it; and I need not say that I had rather any of my sons should be so dignified and distinguished than to have the title of 'His Holiness.'" Although John took over what Charles had started, Charles rejoiced in it, and there was never any bitterness on his part. On John's part, he always spoke of the work that was being done as their joint work. "My brother and I," is the expression he constantly used in describing it. Charles was by no means a mere "man Friday" for his brother, as some have supposed. He would not have been a Wesley if he had not given proof of magnificent individuality. He was the first Methodist, and he was to take his full share in the work of the great revival, not only as a poet, but as a preacher.

John Gambold, one of the original members of the Holy Club, wrote: "Mr. John Wesley was always the chief manager, for which he was very fit; for he not only had more learning and experience than the rest, but he was blest with such activity as to be always gaining ground, and such steadiness that he lost none. What proposals he made to any were sure to charm them, because they saw him always the same. What supported this uniform vigor was the care he took to consider well of every affair before he engaged in it, making all his decisions in the fear of God, without passion, humor, or self-confidence; for though he had naturally a very clear apprehension, yet his exact prudence depended more on

⇒ 18 ⇐

humanity and singleness of heart. To this I may add that he had, I think, something of authority on his countenance; though, as he did not want address, he could soften his manner and point it as occasion required. Yet he never assumed anything to himself above his companions. Any of them might speak their mind, and their words were as strictly regarded by him as his were by them."

The first and foremost work of the Holy Club was the study of the Bible. The new movement was spiritual, humanitarian, but first and foremost scriptural. The searching of the Scriptures was earnest, open-minded, devout, unceasing. Wesley himself said: "From the very beginning—from the time that four young men united together—each of them was a man of one book. They had one, and only one, rule of judgment. They were continually reproached for this very thing, some terming them in derision Bible Bigots; others, Bible Moths; feeding, they said, upon the Bible as moths do on cloth. And indeed, unto this day, it is their constant endeavor to think and speak as the oracles of God."

The first fruit of their Bible study was a new charitable activity. William Morgan, of Christ Church, visited a condemned man in the castle jail who had murdered his wife. Morgan also talked with the debtors in prison, and was convinced that some good work might be done among them. On August 24, 1730, John and Charles went with him to the castle prison, and from that time forward the prisoners became the special care of the Holy Club. Morgan also began visiting the sick. John Wesley wrote to his father for counsel, and received an inspiring letter from him: "I have the highest reason to bless God that he has given me two sons together at Oxford, to whom he has given grace and courage to turn the war against the world and the devil, which is the best way to conquer them."

The Bishop of Oxford gave the young men his approval, and the visiting was extended to poor families in the city. Children were taught not only the Scriptures but what they needed to know to obtain work. A young girl, who was in a great state of poverty, called on John Wesley for help. He said to her, "You seem half starved; have you nothing to cover you but that thin linen gown?"

She replied, "Sir, this is all I have."

Wesley put his hand into his pocket, but found it nearly empty. The walls of his chamber, however, were hung with pictures, and they seemed to accuse him. "It struck me," he says, "Will thy Master say, 'Well done, good and faithful steward? Thou hast adorned thy walls with the money which might have screened this poor creature from the cold! O Justice! O Mercy! Are not these pictures the blood of this poor maid?'"

He said later that it became the practice of all the Oxford Methodists to give away each year all they had after providing for their own necessities. He received thirty pounds one year, lived on twenty-eight, and gave away two. The next year, he received sixty pounds but still lived on twenty-eight and gave away thirty-two. The third year he received ninety pounds and gave away sixty-two. The fourth year he received one hundred and twenty pounds, and still lived on twenty-eight as before, giving to the poor all the rest. He kept up this practice for the rest of his life.

Samuel Wesley had a hard struggle all through his life, and on April 25, 1735, at the age of seventy-two, he laid down his cross and took up his crown. His sons were by his side during his last hours. His mind was at rest, his heart at peace. He said to John, "The inward witness, son, the inward witness—this is the proof, the strongest proof, of Christianity." But it would be some years before John would know much about that. The day before his death Samuel told Charles, "The weaker I am in body the stronger and more sensible support I feel from God." To the question, "Are you in much pain?" he replied: "God does chasten me with pain, yea, all my bones with strong pain. But I thank Him for all, I bless Him for all, I love Him for all." Laying his hands on Charles's head, he said: "Be steady. The Christian faith will surely revive in this kingdom; you shall see it, though I shall not." To his daughter Erailia he said, "Do not be concerned at my death; God will then begin to manifest himself to my family." He died peacefully just before sunset, and was buried "very frugally, yet decently, in the churchyard, according to his own desire."

Although the Holy Club never exceeded twenty-seven members, many of them made significant spiritual contributions, in addition to those of Charles and John Wesley. John Gambold later became a Moravian bishop. John Clayton became a distinguished Anglican churchman. James Hervey became a noted religious writer. Benjamin Ingham became a Yorkshire evangelist. Thomas Brougham became secretary of the SPCK.* George Whitefield, who joined the club just before the Wesleys departed for Georgia, was associated with Jonathan Edwards in the Great Awakening in America, and with the Evangelical Revival in England. Looking back from 1781, John Wesley saw in the Holy Club the "first rise" of Methodism. The "second rise" came about when he was in Georgia in 1736. He started meeting with selected members of his congregation on Sunday afternoons. From these meetings came the idea for "Methodist societies" that became the backbone of the Methodist organization.

(*The Society for Promoting Christian Knowledge (earlier known as the Society for the Propagation of Christian Knowledge and more commonly known as SPCK) is the oldest Anglican mission organization. It was founded in 1698 by Thomas Bray (an Anglican priest), and a small group of friends. It is now most widely known for being a chain of bookshops in the UK specializing in Christian books.)

In the area of evangelism and revivals, the Holy Club had one member who was exceptional in both, along with the Wesley brothers—although in some places in the world his fame exceeded theirs. His name was George Whitefield.

George Whitefield was the son of an innkeeper at Gloucester, and drew ale for the customers until he was fifteen years of age. At the school to which he was sent he created a considerable stir with his talent for public speaking and acting. He ardently read all of the writings of Thomas à Kempis, and began to dream of being a minister. At eighteen he entered Pembroke College, Oxford, as a servitor, for which his bartending experience served him well. He was drawn to the Holy Club, but because of his extreme poverty he was afraid to ask if he could join the young noblemen who made up the club. He often watched them with deep emotion, however, as they passed through a jeering crowd to receive the sacrament at St. Mary's. At length he made the acquaintance of Charles Wesley, who gave him religious counsel and helpful books. These created a deep hunger that culminated in a powerful religious experience.

Whitefield learned that true religion did not consist in going to church, or in faithfulness in any external duties, but was a union of the soul with God; and that he must be a new creature. It was a turning point in his spiritual history. He said: "I found and felt in myself that I was delivered from the burden that had so heavily oppressed me. The spirit of mourning was taken from me, and I knew what it was truly to rejoice in God my Savior. The daystar arose in my heart. I know the place; it may perhaps be superstitious, but whenever I go to Oxford I cannot help running to the spot where Jesus Christ first revealed himself to me and gave me a new birth."

His "new birth" was in 1735, when he was in his twenty-first year. He was the first of the Holy Club to come into this born-again experience. Why he did not at once tell the Wesley brothers, who for three years continued to grope in the darkness of legalism, may be partly due to their superior education and social position. He perhaps felt it would be presumptuous on his part to teach them about this new birth. There is also the great possibility that his silence was due to the fact that they became at this time separated from him by their preparations for departure to America. So the two Wesleys went on their way without yet experiencing the great doctrines of justification by faith and the witness of the Spirit to their spirit that they were children of God. Eventually they would learn what was necessary in order to experience true salvation, not from any great teacher within their own church, but from the lips of a humble Moravian preacher, and from the glowing commentaries of the great German reformer, Martin Luther.

———•·•———

In 1732, a royal charter was granted for the establishment of a colony, named after King George, "in that part of Carolina which lies from the most northern part of the Savannah River all along the seacoast to the southward." The founder was General James Edward Oglethorpe, an energetic and humanitarian member of Parliament. Four groups had migrated to that area; the Wesleys and their party would be part of the fifth migration.—Ray Comfort

———•·•———

In the summer of 1735, when the Georgian trustees were looking for a missionary, someone suggested John Wesley, the zealous young fellow of Lincoln. General Oglethorpe liked the idea, but John doubted whether his widowed mother could spare him. He finally went home to ask her. "Had I twenty sons," was her noble reply, "I should rejoice that they were all so employed, though I should never see them more." Charles decided to go as the general's secretary; and Benjamin Ingham of the Holy Club, and a young Londoner named Delamotte joined the mission, for that's what they considered it.

Wesley's motives for going, however, are best learned from his own candid words in a letter to a friend. The apparent selfishness of his first, or chief, motive is probably better judged in light of his second motive. He apparently believed that in order to fulfill his second motive, he first needed to experience the hope of his first motive. "My chief motive," he said, "is the hope of saving my own soul. I hope to learn the true sense of the Gospel of Christ by preaching it to the heathen. They have no comments to construe away the text; no vain philosophy to corrupt it; no luxurious, sensual, covetous, ambitious expounders to soften its unpleasing truths ...They have no party, no interest to serve, and are therefore fit to receive the Gospel in its simplicity. They are as little children, humble, willing to learn, and eager to do the will of God.

"I then hope to know what it is to love my neighbor as myself, and to feel the powers of that second motive to visit the heathen, even the desire to impart to them what I have received—a saving knowledge of the Gospel of Christ; but this I dare not think on yet. It is not for me, who have been a grievous sinner from my youth up ... to expect God should work so great things by my hands; but I am assured, if I be once converted myself, he will then employ me both to strengthen my brethren and to preach his name to the Gentiles."

On October 18, 1735, the party of "missioners" embarked with General Oglethorpe on the Simmonds, a sailing vessel of two hundred and twenty tons. Aboard were twenty-six Moravians under their bishop David Nitsehman, and eighty English colonists.

Although they started from Gravesend, a town in northwest Kent, England, in October, it was December before they actually left England, because they had to spend many weeks at Cowes, on the Isle of Wight, which is an English island and county off the southern English coast. There they had to wait for a man-of-war that was to be their convoy to the Americas. This gave the Methodists time to plan their days as carefully as at Oxford. From four to five every morning was spent in private prayer; then they read the Bible together for two hours, comparing it with the writings of the Church Fathers. Breakfast and public prayers filled two hours more.

From nine to twelve Charles Wesley wrote sermons, John studied German, Delamotte read Greek, and Ingham taught the emigrants' children. The remainder of the day was as carefully mapped out. In the evening, they joined the Germans in their evening service.

There was one event during the eight weeks' voyage that made a deep impression on John Wesley. On several occasions there were severe storms that tossed their small vessel about like a toy. When it did, John was terrified and realized that he was afraid to die. He had made friends with the Moravians and was charmed by their sweet spirit and excellent discipline. He now found that they were as brave as they were gentle. One evening a violent storm broke upon the vessel just as the Moravians began to sing a psalm. The wind split the mainsail into shreds and a huge wave rolled over the ship, covering it and pouring water down into the lower decks as if the sea were swallowing them up. The English began to scream with terror, but the Moravians calmly sang on as if nature wasn't roaring in fury all about them.

After the storm passed, Wesley asked one of the Moravian leaders, "Were you not afraid?"

"I thank God, no," was the reply.

"But," John said, "were not your women and children afraid?"

"No," the Moravian replied mildly, "Our women and children are not afraid to die."

At the close of the day, Wesley wrote in his journal, "This was the most glorious day which I have hitherto seen."

On February 6, 1736, the Simmonds landed her passengers in Georgia. One of Wesley's first acquaintances was a man named Spangenberg, a Moravian pastor whose advice he sought about dealing with the heathens. But rather than answer his questions, the pastor said to him, "My brother, I must first ask you one or two questions: Have you the witness within yourself? Does the Spirit of God witness with your spirit that you are a child of God?"

Wesley did not know what to answer. The pastor, seeing his hesitation, asked, "Do you know Jesus Christ?"

"I know that He is the Savior of the world," Wesley said.

"True," the pastor said, "but do you know He has saved you?" Wesley answered, "I hope He has died to save me."

"But do you know yourself?" the pastor asked.

"I do," was John's reply. But in his Journal he wrote, "I fear they were vain words."

John had never received such a spiritual probing before. The conversation was worth his journey across the ocean. But though so close to the light, he still remained in darkness. He visited Pastor Spangenberg many times and asked him many questions about the Moravians of Herrnhut, Germany.

Charles Wesley was sent home in 1736 with dispatches for the governor and never returned to Georgia, but John stayed there for nearly two years. Neither of them experienced much success. John's High Church Christianity was so legalistic that it repulsed more people than it drew. He rejected a Presbyterian minister's advice to consider his parishioners as babes in their progress, and to feed them with milk. Instead, "he drenched them with the physic of an intolerant discipline." One plain-speaking Christian said to him, "The people say they are Protestants, but as for you, they cannot tell what religion you are of; they never heard of such a religion before, and they do not know what to make of it."

The incident that ended John Wesley's usefulness as a missionary had to do with a young lady with whom he fell deeply in love. Her name was Sophia Hopkey. She was the niece of the chief magistrate of Savannah, and highly attractive. They were close to being engaged to be married, but on the advice of his Moravian friends John suddenly decided not to marry her, and she soon married another man. The attachment must have been very strong, for in his old age he wrote of his feeling at her marrying someone else, "I was pierced through as with a sword."

But the matter did not end here. Later Wesley felt it was his duty to rebuke Sophia for what he considered her inconsistency of life and to refuse her the privilege of receiving Communion. He was prosecuted by her husband for so doing, but as a High Churchman he refused to recognize the authority of a civil court. Then the backlash burst upon him. The colonists found many grievances against their legalistic and rigid minister. He sought advice from some of his friends, and to end the matter he decided to leave Georgia. So on December 5, 1737, he boarded a ship with three friends for Carolina. After a difficult journey of ten days they reached Charleston, and went on board the Samuel. After a stormy voyage, Wesley rejoiced to see "English land once more; which, about noon, appeared to be the Lizard Point," and the next day, February 1, 1738, they landed at Deal in Kent, England.

On his voyage home, Wesley poured out his soul in his Journal: "I went to America to convert the Indians, but, O! Who shall convert me? Who, what is he that will deliver me from this evil heart of unbelief? I have a fair summer religion; I can talk well, nay, and believe myself, while no danger is near; but let death look me in the face, and my spirit is troubled. Nor can I say, to die is gain … I show my faith by my works, by staking my all upon it. I would do so again and again a thousand times, if the choice were still to make. Whoever sees me sees I would be a Christian … But in a storm I think, *What if the Gospel be not true? … O who will deliver me from this fear of death? … Where shall I fly from it?*"

The day that he landed in England at Deal, there was another gloomy entry in his Journal, but he ends it by looking toward the light that started to shine in Georgia. "This, then, have I learned in the ends of the earth, that I am fallen short of the glory of God; that my whole heart is altogether corrupt and abominable … that my own works, my own sufferings, my own righteousness, are so far from reconciling me to an offended God, that the most specious of them need an atonement themselves ... that, 'having the sentence of death' in my heart ... I have no hope ... but that if I seek, I shall find Christ, and 'be found in him, not having my own righteousness, but that which is through the faith of Christ, the righteousness which is of God by faith.' I want ... that faith which enables every one that hath it to cry out, 'I live not ... but Christ liveth in me; and the life which I now live, I live by faith in the Son of God, who loved me, and gave himself for me.' I want that faith which none can have without knowing he hath it; when 'the Spirit itself beareth witness with his spirit that he is a child of God.'" (Romans 8:16 reads: "The Spirit itself beareth witness with our spirit, that we are the children of God.")

For several years after they returned from Georgia, the Wesleys were in almost constant contact with certain Moravians whose teachings kept alive the doctrine of justification by faith. One of them, Peter Bohler, wrote to Count Zinzendorf, the founder and leader of the Moravians, at Herrnhut about his association with them and their knowledge of salvation by faith. "I traveled with the two brothers, John and Charles Wesley, from London to Oxford. The elder, John, is a good-natured man; he knew he did not properly believe on the Savior, and was willing to be taught. His brother, with whom you often conversed a year ago, is at present very much distressed in his mind, but does not know how he shall begin to be acquainted with the Savior. Our mode of believing in the Savior is so easy to Englishmen that they cannot reconcile themselves to it; if it were a little more artful [requiring skill to achieve], they would much sooner find their way into it. Of faith in Jesus they have no other idea than the generality [majority] of people have. They justify themselves; and therefore they always take it for granted that they believe already, and try to prove their faith by their works, and thus so plague and torment themselves that they are at heart very miserable."

On Sunday, March 5, 1738, John Wesley wrote: "I was, in the hand of the great God, clearly convinced of unbelief, of the want [lack] of that faith whereby alone we are saved." Because of his spiritual condition, he asked Bohler if he should stop preaching salvation, to which his friend replied, "By no means."

"But what can I preach?" Wesley asked him.

Bohler replied, "Preach faith till you have it, and then because you have it you will preach faith."

So on Monday morning Wesley preached salvation by faith to a man under sentence of death in Oxford Castle. When he visited the condemned man hours later, he was deeply moved when the man rose from prayer exclaiming eagerly, "I am now ready to die. I know Christ has taken away my sins, and there is no more condemnation for me." He continued to proclaim his salvation until his voice was silenced by the hangman's noose.

To help John Wesley and others in the Holy Club, Bohler brought together some Moravian friends to testify of their salvation by faith. As they testified with clarity and passion to the joy of faith and the inner witness of the Spirit, John Wesley and his Methodist companions were "as if thunderstruck." The Moravians ended their testimonies by singing an old Moravian hymn, "My Soul Before Thee Prostrate Lies."
John Wesley's many conversations with Bohler, the salvation testimony of the Moravians, and the singing of their old hymn filled him with a conviction that he had never had before. He

wrote: "I was now thoroughly convinced; and, by the grace of God, I resolved to seek it unto the end: (1) By absolutely renouncing all dependence, in whole or in part, upon my own works or righteousness; on which I had really grounded my hope of salvation, though I knew it not, from my youth up. (2) By adding to the constant use of all the other means of grace, continual prayer for this very thing, justifying, saving faith, a full reliance on the blood of Christ shed for me; a trust in him as my Christ, as my sole justification, sanctification, and redemption."

Within weeks his new determination bore fruit. On Wednesday, May 24, 1738, at five in the morning, he opened his New Testament to 2 Peter 1:4 and read these words: "Whereby are given unto us exceeding great and precious promises: that by these ye might be partakers of the divine nature." As he was leaving his house that morning, his New Testament open in his hand, he saw these words in Mark 12:34:"Thou art not far from the kingdom of God."

That same evening he went "very unwillingly" to a meeting in Nettleton Court, on the east side of Aldersgate Street, where a few Christians and seekers met for prayer and Bible study. A Moravian was reading Luther's Preface to the Epistle to the Romans, in which Luther speaks of trying to obtain salvation by the works of the law and the true salvation that is only by faith. "At about a quarter before nine o'clock while he [Luther in his Preface] was describing the change which God works in the heart through faith in Christ, I felt my heart strangely warmed. I felt I did trust in Christ, Christ alone, for salvation; and an assurance was given me that he had taken away my sins, even mine, and saved me from the law of sin and death. I began to pray with all my might for those who had in a more especial manner despitefully used me and persecuted me. I then testified openly to all there what I now first felt in my heart."

The house of Mr. Bray, a brazier, where Charles was staying to regain his health, was but a few steps away, and John hurried there and greeted his brother with the rapturous words, "I believe." They then sang a new hymn that Charles had composed just a few weeks previous: "Where Shall My Wondering Soul Begin?"

John Wesley's conversion revolutionized the whole character and method of his ministry. The great evangelical doctrines of justification by faith had been obscured by his High Church legalism. His moral teachings, pious as they were, had not been inspired by the only motives that matter—the love and glory of God, and God's saving love toward humanity.

For many years Wesley had worked for God as a servant, but now by faith he had become a son; and from this moment, as Dr. Rigg [unknown] wrote, "this ritualistic priest and ecclesiastical martinet was to be transformed into a flaming preacher of the great evangelical salvation and life in all its branches, and its rich and varied experiences. Hence arose Wesleyan Methodism and all the Methodist Churches."

Rev. Hugh Price Hughes (1847–1902), the British Nonconformist and Methodist divine, expressed a similar conviction about the historical importance of Wesley's conversion: "The Rubicon was crossed. The sweeping aside of ecclesiastical traditions, the rejection of the apostolical succession, the ordination with his own hands of presbyters and bishops, the final organization of a separate and fully equipped Church, were all logically involved in what took place that night."

Over many years God had prepared his man, and now He brought him into full sonship and put a holy fire in him that would set all of England aflame with the glory and power of God. It was a fire that would burn white-hot within John Wesley until his death on March 2, 1791.

Illustration Portfolio

JOHN WESLEY
AN ETCHING AFTER A 1788 PORTRAIT BY WILLIAM HAMILTON.

ILLUSTRATION BY FRANCES ARTHUR FRASER OF
JOHN AND CHARLES WESLEY AT BRISTOL—
SITE OF THE FOUNDING OF THE FIRST METHODIST CHAPEL.

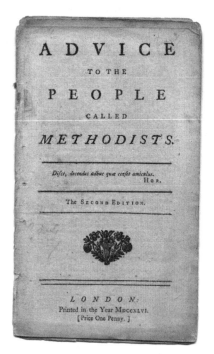

WESLEY TRACT.

CHARLES WESLEY

Wesley preaching open-air in Cornwell, England.

ENGRAVING OF JOHN WESLEY AND GEORGE WHITEFIELD PREACHING
ABOUT THE NEW JERUSALEM.

PORTRAIT OF A YOUNG JOHN WESLEY.

Various portraits of John Wesley.

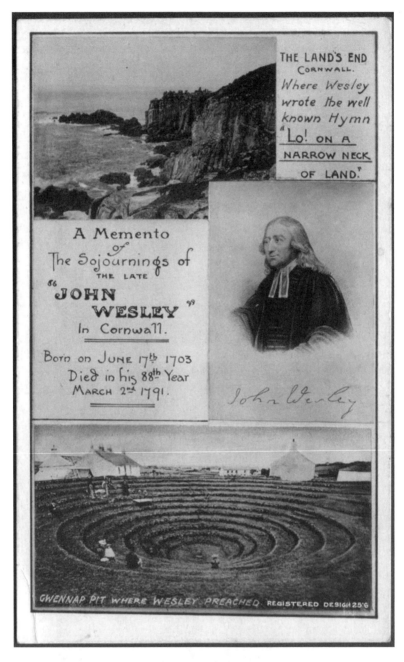

A MEMENTO OF THE SOJOURNINGS OF JOHN WESLEY IN CORNWELL,
WHERE HE WROTE THE HYMN "LO! ON A NARROW NECK OF LAND."

Wesley on his deathbed, writing William Wilberforce.

STATUE OF WESLEY AT AOYAMA GAKUIN UNIVERSITY IN TOKYO, JAPAN,
FOUNDED IN 1874 BY THE METHODIST EPISCOPAL CHURCH OF THE
UNITED STATES.

STATUE OF JOHN WESLEY AND HIS HOUSE AT SHOREDITCH, ENGLAND, BUILT IN 1779.

Wesley's Stature

L ike the others of the Epworth family, John Wesley was small in stature. Barely five feet six and weighing only one hundred and twenty-two pounds, he was yet muscular and strong. Bright hazel eyes, fine features, an aquiline nose, a fine forehead, and a clear complexion combined to make his face arresting. Contemporaries have said that his eyes retained their bright and penetrating quality even to his last years.

This is a great encouragement for those who lack an imposing stature. It's ironic that being of small stature can be an advantage in open air preaching. I'm about Wesley's height, and many times I have had people threaten to hit me and I have said to them, "You've got to be kidding. Look at me. Hit me and you will turn the crowd against you." That has caused them to back off. I have a long-standing friend who is just under seven feet tall. Before he was a Christian, Hank (who is a gentle giant) said that he was often beaten up in bars by drunks. Big men are tall trees to topple--a big challenge. Little folks are more like twigs.—Ray Comfort

The Journal of John Wesley, John Wesley (Appreciation of the Journal by Augustine Birrell, K.C., Moody Press (Chicago). ISBN: 0-8024-4390-7. Edited by Percy Livingstone Parker, page 25

A Captive Audience

In pursuance of [his] directions, I immediately went to Mr. Gerard, the Bishop of Oxford's chaplain, who was likewise the person that took care of the prisoners when any were condemned to die (at other times they were left to their own care); I proposed to him our design of serving them as far as we could and my own intention to preach there once a month, if the bishop approved of it. He much commended our design and said he would answer for the bishop's approbation, to whom he would take the first opportunity of mentioning it. It was not long before he informed me he had done so and that his lordship not only gave his permission, but was greatly pleased with the undertaking and hoped it would have the desired success.

Soon after, a gentleman of Merton College, who was one of our little company which now consisted of five persons, acquainted us that he had been much rallied the day before for being a member of the Holy Club; and that it was become a common topic of mirth at his college, where they had found out several of our customs, to which we were ourselves utter strangers. Upon this I consulted my father again.

Upon [his] encouragement we still continued to meet together as usual; and to confirm one another, as well as we could, in our resolutions to communicate as often as we had opportunity (which is here once a week); and do what service we could to our acquaintance, the prisoners, and two or three poor families in the town.

The Journal of John Wesley, John Wesley (Appreciation of the Journal by Augustine Birrell, K.C., Moody Press (Chicago). ISBN: 0-8024-4390-7. Edited by Percy Livingstone Parker, page 32

Wesley's Discipline

We now began to be a little regular. Our common way of living was this: From four in the morning till five each of us used private prayer. From five to seven we read the Bible together, carefully comparing it (that we might not lean to our own understandings) with the writing of the earliest ages. At seven we breakfasted. At eight were the public prayers. From nine to twelve I usually learned German, and Mr. Delamotte, Greek. My brother wrote sermons, and Mr. Ingham instructed the children. At twelve we met to give an account of one another—what we had done since our last meeting, and what we designed to do before our next. About one we dined.

The Journal of John Wesley, John Wesley (Appreciation of the Journal by Augustine Birrell, K.C., Moody Press (Chicago). ISBN: 0-8024-4390-7. Edited by Percy Livingstone Parker, page 33

It is amazing to think that with all this discipled prayer and Bible reading, Wesley was not saved at this point in his life. He was still trusting in his works to save him.

A 2004 Barna Poll found that "five out of ten believe a person can earn salvation based on good deeds even without accepting Christ as the way to eternal life."—Ray Comfort

---

The Awakening Storm

A bout nine the sea broke over us from stern to stern; burst through the windows of the state cabin, where three or four of us were, and covered us all over, though a bureau sheltered me from the main shock. About eleven I lay down in a great cabin and in a short time fell asleep, though very uncertain whether I should wake alive and much ashamed of my unwillingness to die. Oh, how pure in heart must he be, who would rejoice to appear before God at a moment's warning! Toward morning "He rebuked the winds and the sea; and there was a great calm" [Matt. 8:26]

This is the famous storm where Wesley found that he lacked assurance of salvation. —Ray Comfort

---

SUNDAY, 25 – At noon our third storm began. At four it was more violent than before. At seven I went to the Germans. I had long before observed the great seriousness of their behavior. Of their humility they had given a continual proof by performing those servile offices for the other passengers, which none of the English would undertake; for which they desired and would receive no pay, saying, "it was good for their proud hearts," and "their loving Savior had done more for them." And every day had given them an occasion of showing a meekness which no injury could move. If they were pushed, struck, or thrown down, they rose again and went away; but no complaint was found in their mouth.

There was now an opportunity of trying whether they were delivered from the spirit of fear, as well as from that of pride, anger and revenge. In the midst of the psalm wherewith their service began, the sea broke over, split the mainsail in pieces, covered the ship, and poured in between the decks, as if the great deep had already swallowed us up. A terrible screaming began among the English. The Germans calmly sang on. I asked one of them afterward, "Were you not afraid?" He answered, "I thank God, no." I asked, "But were not your women and children afraid?" He replied, mildly, "No; our women and children are not afraid to die."

Saturday, 7 – Mr. Oglethorpe returned from Savannah with Mr. Spangenberg, one of the pastors of the Germans. I soon found what spirit he was of and asked his advice with regard to my own conduct. He said, "My brother, I must first ask you one or two questions. Have you the witness within yourself? Does the Spirit of God bear witness with your spirit that you are a child of God?" I was surprised, and knew not what to answer. He observed it and asked, "Do you know Jesus Christ?" I paused and said, "I know He is the Savior of the world." "True," replied he; "but do you know He has saved you?" I answered, "I hope He has died to save me." He only added, "Do you know yourself?" I said, "I do." But I fear they were vain words.

The Journal of John Wesley, John Wesley (Appreciation of the Journal by Augustine Birrell, K.C., Moody Press (Chicago). ISBN: 0-8024-4390-7. Edited by Percy Livingstone Parker, page 35-37

Who Shall Convert Me?

Tuesday, 24 – We spoke with two ships, outward bound, from whom we had the welcome news of our wanting but one hundred and sixty leagues of the Land's End. My mind was now full of thought; part of which I wrote down as follows:

"I went to America, to convert the Indians; but oh! Who shall convert me? Who, what is he that will deliver me from this evil heart of mischief? I have a fair summer religion. I can talk well; nay, and believe myself, while no danger is near; but let death look me in the face, and my spirit is troubled. Nor can I say, 'To die is gain!'

I have a sin of fear, that when I've spun my last thread, I shall perish on the shore!

"I think, verily, if the gospel be true, I am safe: for I not only have given, and do give, all my goods to feed the poor; I not only give my body to be burned, drowned, or whatever God shall appoint for me; but I follow after charity (though not as I ought, yet as I can), if haply I may attain it. I now believe the gospel is true. 'I show my faith by my works,' by staking my all upon it. I would do so again and again a thousand times, if the choice were still to make."

The Journal of John Wesley, John Wesley (Appreciation of the Journal by Augustine Birrell, K.C., Moody Press (Chicago). ISBN: 0-8024-4390-7. Edited by Percy Livingstone Parker, page 53

Words of Truth and Soberness

It is now two years and almost four months since I left my native country in order to teach the Georgian Indians the nature of Christianity. But what have I learned in the meantime? Why (what I the least of all suspected), that I who went to America to convert others was never myself converted to God. "I am not mad," though I thus speak; but "I speak the words of truth and soberness"; if haply some of those who still dream may awake and see that as I am, so are they.

The Journal of John Wesley, John Wesley (Appreciation of the Journal by Augustine Birrell, K.C., Moody Press (Chicago). ISBN: 0-8024-4390-7. Edited by Percy Livingstone Parker, page 54-55

The Offense of Truth

Accordingly, the next morning I waited on Mr. Oglethorpe but had not time to speak on that head. In the afternoon I was desired to preach at St. John the Evangelist's. I did so on those strong words, "If any man be in Christ, he is a new creature" [II Corinthians. 5:17]. I was afterward informed many of the best in the parish were so offended that I was not to preach there any more.

Ibid, page 56

A Change of Mind

Immediately it struck into my mind, "Leave off preaching. How can you preach to others, who have not faith yourself?" I asked Bohler whether he thought I should leave it off or not. He answered, "By no means." I asked, "But what can I preach?" He said, "Preach faith till you have it, and then, because you have it, you will preach faith."

According, Monday, 6, I began preaching this new doctrine, though my soul started back from the work. The first person to whom I offered salvation by faith alone was a prisoner under sentence of death. His name was Clifford. Peter Bohler had many times desired me to speak to him before. But I could not prevail on myself so to do; being still, as I had been many years, a zealous asserter of the impossibility of a deathbed repentance.

Most works-based beliefs deny deathbed salvations. I often ask cults such as Jehovah's Witnesses and Mormons what they can do for me if I have a knife in my back, and only three minutes to live. They preach that a man or woman is saved by works, and they become flustered. They usually end up saying that nothing can be done in that case. It reveals their false doctrine. They deny salvation by grace alone through faith alone. See Ephesians 2:8-9.—*Ray Comfort*

The Journal of John Wesley, John Wesley (Appreciation of the Journal by Augustine Birrell, K.C., Moody Press (Chicago). ISBN: 0-8024-4390-7. Edited by Percy Livingstone Parker, page 58.

Open Air preaching

THURSDAY, MARCH 29 – I left London and in the evening expounded to a small company at Basingstoke. Saturday, 31. In the evening I reached Bristol and met Mr. Whitefield there. I could scarcely reconcile myself at first to this strange way of preaching in the fields, of which he set me an example on Sunday; I had been all my life (till very lately) so tenacious of every point relating to decency and order that I should have thought the saving of souls almost a sin if it had not been done in a church.

This was the beginning of Wesley's understanding of the effectiveness of open air preaching. This statement is strange in itself. I often wonder myself how anyone can be amazed by preaching in the open air because it was what John the Baptist, Jesus, Stephen, Paul and so many others did in Scripture. If anything, standing behind a pulpit and preaching to people in pews should be strange to us. If you are also a stranger to open air preaching, see our Four-in-One Open Air Preaching DVD at www.livingwaters. com—Ray Comfort

You Are Beside Yourself

APRIL 1 – In the evening (Mr. Whitefield being gone) I began expounding our Lord's Sermon on the Mount (one pretty remarkable precedent of field-preaching, though I suppose there were churches at that time also), to a little society which was accustomed to meet once or twice a week in Nicholas Street.

MONDAY, 2 – At four in the afternoon, I submitted to be more vile and proclaimed in the highways the glad tidings of salvation, speaking from a little eminence in a ground adjoining to the city, to about three thousand people. The Scripture on which I spoke was this (is it possible anyone should be ignorant that it is fulfilled in every true minister of Christ?): "The Spirit of the Lord is upon me, because he hath anointed me to preach the gospel to the poor; he hath sent me to heal the brokenhearted, to preach deliverance to the captives, and recovering of sight to the blind, to set at liberty them that are bruised, to preach the acceptable year of the Lord" [see Isaiah. 61:1, 2; Luke 4:18, 19].

SUNDAY, 8 – At seven in the morning I preached to about a thousand persons at Bristol, and afterward to about fifteen hundred on the top of Hannam Mount in Kingswood. I called to them, in the words of the evangelical prophet, "Ho! every one that thirsteth, come ye to the waters ... come, buy wine and milk without money and without price" [Isaiah. 55:1]. About five thousand were in the afternoon at Rose Green (on the other side of Kingswood); among whom I stood and cried in the name of the Lord, "If any man thirst, let him come unto me and drink. He that believeth on me, as the Scripture hath said, out of his belly shall flow rivers of living water" [John 7:37, 38] . Ibid, page 67-68

MONDAY, MAY 7 – I was preparing to set out for Pensford, having now had leave to preach in the church, when I received the following note:

"Sir, Our minister, having been informed you are beside yourself, does not care that you should preach in any of his churches." I went, however; and on Priestdown, about half a mile from Pensford, preached Christ our "wisdom, righteousness, sanctification, and redemption."
Ibid, page 68-69

———————

The assertion was that Wesley was insane. The same thing was said of his Master.—Ray Comfort

Warning Them

SUNDAY, 20 – Seeing many of the rich at Clifton Church, my heart was much pained for them and I was earnestly desirous that some even of them might "enter into the kingdom of heaven." But full as I was, I knew not where to begin in warning them to flee from the wrath to come till my Testament opened on these words: "I came not to call the righteous, but sinners to repentance" [Mark 2:17]; in applying which my soul was so enlarged that I thought I could have cried out in another sense than poor vain Archimedes, "Give me where

to stand, and I will shake the earth." God's sending forth lightning with the rain did not hinder about fifteen hundred from staying at Rose Green. Our Scripture was, "It is the glorious God that maketh the thunder. The voice of the LORD is mighty in operation; the voice of the LORD is a glorious voice" [see Psalms. 29: 3, 4]. In the evening He spoke to three whose souls were all storm and tempest, and immediately there was a great calm.
Ibid, page 70

This is a dilemma for most of us, because wrath is the essence of our message. Yet it isn't what the world wants to hear. But we must speak of sin for the cross to make sense and sin and judgment go hand in hand. To preach Christ crucified without the warning to flee from wrath is to betray our hearers. The cross makes no sense if God isn't angry at sin. I once watched in horror as a small dog wandered onto the middle of a busy road and began sniffing something. Suddenly a police car pulled to the side of the road and the officer inside began to honk his horn at the dog. Cars stopped at the sound of the horn. The animal was frightened by the horn but not enough to stop sniffing immediately. The dumb animal kept sniffing for a moment and then quickly ran off the road. The gospel is a warning. It sounds an alarm to the sinner to stop sniffing the filth of sin, and immediately get off the road before the vehicle of eternal justice grinds him to powder. Our dilemma is to make the sinner's immediate and terrible danger make sense to him. As Wesley knew and preached, it is the Law that makes judgment reasonable.—Ray Comfort

---

How wonderful it is to hear a massive roll of thunder and a flash of lightning. Such things tend to put the fear of God into our hearers.—Ray Comfort

TUESDAY, JUNE 5 – There was great expectation at Bath of what a noted man was to do to me there; and I was much entreated not to preach because no one knew what might happen. By this report I also gained a much larger audience, among whom were many of the rich and great. I told them plainly the Scripture had concluded them all under sin—high and low, rich and poor, one with another. Many of them seemed to be a little surprised and were sinking apace into seriousness, when their champion appeared and, coming close to me, asked by what authority I did these things.

———•••———

The modern "Jesus will make you happy" message isn't relevant to those who are rich and happy. However, the biblical gospel is universal.—Ray Comfort

If you ever open air preach, be ready for these folks. They will often begin by asking what good it does to "yell" at people in the open. They will usually accuse you of being unloving. Their real mission is to discourage you from preaching to the lost. Be gentle. Be respectful. And don't be discouraged.—Ray Comfort

———•••———

I replied, "By the authority of Jesus Christ, conveyed to me by the (now) Archbishop of Canterbury, when he laid hands upon me and said, 'Take thou authority to preach the gospel.'" He said, "This is contrary to the Act of Parliament: this is a conventicle." I answered, "Sir, the conventicles mentioned in the Act (as the preamble shows are seditious meetings); but this is not such; here is no shadow of sedition; therefore it is not contrary to that Act." He replied, "I say it is: and beside, your preaching frightens people out of their wits."

Our preaching should put the fear of God in our listeners. Hell is a fearful thing. Besides, there is such a thing as a fear that is there for our good. Fear stops us stepping off cliffs, walking into fire, etc. This beneficial fear is produced when the Law is used to bring the knowledge of sin. It bears witness with the conscience and shows that God's judgment is just, and that we are justly damned. It was this fear that made Felix tremble as he heard Paul preach sin, temperance and judgment. His heart trembled. See Acts 24:25.—Ray Comfort

"Sir, did you ever hear me preach?" "No." "How then can you judge of what you never heard?" "Sir, by common report." "Common report is not enough. Give me leave, Sir, to ask, Is not your name Nash?" "My name is Nash." "Sir, I dare not judge of you by common report: I think it not enough to judge by." Here he paused awhile and, having recovered himself, said, "I desire to know what this people comes here for;" on which one replied, "Sir, leave him to me; let an old woman answer. You, Mr. Nash, take care of our body; we take care of our souls; and for the food of our souls we come here." He replied not a word, but walked away.

*Often these folks will speak up from the midst of a crowd (who are there by their own free choice, and say something like, "You are deceiving these people!" I usually reply, "And you have stepped up on behalf of these poor sheep as their intellectual savior. You think they are so dumb that they haven't the brains to walk away if they hear something with which they don't agree. Sir, these people aren't stupid. If they don't like what they hear they are free to walk away."
—Ray Comfort*

The World is My Parish

I look upon all the world as my parish; thus far I mean, that, in whatever part of it I am, I judge it meet, right, and my bounden duty to declare unto all that are willing to hear, the glad tidings of salvation. This is the work which I know God has called me to; and sure I am that His blessing attends it. Great encouragement have I, therefore, to be faithful in fulfilling the work He has given me to do. His servant I am, and, as such, am employed according to the plain direction of His Word, 'As I have opportunity, doing good unto all men;' and His providence clearly concurs with His Word, which has disengaged me from all things else, that I might singly attend on this very thing, 'and go about doing good.'"

This is perhaps Wesley's most famous saying. However, each of us should have this mindset. We live in a mission field.—Ray Comfort

Whitefield Asks Wesley to Preach

THURSDAY, 14 – I went with Mr. Whitefield to Blackheath, where were, I believe, twelve or fourteen thousand people. He a little surprised me by desiring me to preach in his stead; which I did (though nature recoiled) on my favorite subject, "Jesus Christ, who of God is made unto us wisdom, righteousness, sanctification, and redemption."

I was greatly moved with compassion for the rich that were there, to whom I made a particular application. Some of them seemed to attend, while others drove away their coaches from so uncouth a preacher.

SUNDAY, 17 – I preached at seven in Upper Moorfields to (I believe) six or seven thousand people, on, "Ho, every one that thirsts, come ye to the waters."

MONDAY, 18 – I left London early in the morning and the next evening reached Bristol and preached (as I had appointed, if God should permit) to a numerous congregation. My text now also was "Look unto me, and be ye saved, all the ends of the earth" [Isaiah 45:22]. Howell Harris called upon me an hour or two after. He said he had been much dissuaded from either hearing or seeing me by many who said all manner of evil of me. "But," said he, "as soon as I heard you preach, I quickly found what spirit you were of. And before you had done, I was so overpowered with joy and love that I had much ado to walk home."

FRIDAY, JULY 6 – In the afternoon I was with Mr. Whitefield, just come from London, with whom I went to Baptist Mills, where he preached concerning "the Holy Ghost, which all who believe are to receive"; not without a just, though severe, censure of those who preach as if there were no Holy Ghost.

SATURDAY, 7 – I had an opportunity to talk with him of those outward signs which had so often accompanied the inward work of God. I found his objections were chiefly grounded on gross misrepresentations of matter of fact. But the next day he had an opportunity of informing himself better: for no sooner had he begun (in the application of his sermon) to invite all sinners to believe in Christ, than four persons sank down close to him, almost in the same moment. One of them lay without either sense or motion. A second trembled exceedingly. The third had strong convulsions all over his body, but made no noise unless by groans. The fourth, equally convulsed, called upon God with strong cries and tears. From this time, I trust, we shall all allow God to carry on His own work in the way that pleases Him.   Ibid, page 75-76

———•◦•———

These can sometimes be emotional outbursts that have nothing to do with God. However, when the gospel is preached in truth and strange happens of this nature take place, when there has been no emotional stirring of the crowds, we must have the attitude of Wesley.—Ray Comfort

———•◦•———

SUNDAY, 9 – I declared to about ten thousand, in Moorfields, what they must do to be saved. My mother went with us, about five, to Kennington, where were supposed to be twenty thousand people. I again insisted on that foundation of all our hope, "Believe in the Lord Jesus, and thou shalt be saved." From Kennington I went to a society at Lambeth. The house being filled, the rest stood in the garden. The deep attention they showed gave me a good hope that they will not all be forgetful hearers.

SUNDAY, 16 – I preached at Moorfields to about ten thousand, and at Kennington Common to, I believe, nearly twenty thousand, on those words of the calmer Jews to St. Paul, "We desire to hear of you what you think: for as concerning this sect, we know that everywhere it is spoken against" [Acts 28:22]. At both places I described the real difference between what is generally called Christianity and the true old Christianity, which, under the new name of Methodism, is now also everywhere spoken against.

We have a similar attitude towards Christianity and what the world distains as "fundamentalism."—Ray Comfort

---

SUNDAY, 23 – I declared to about ten thousand, in Moorfields, with great enlargement of spirit, "The kingdom of God is not meat and drink; but righteousness, and peace, and joy in the Holy Ghost" [Romans. 14:17]. At Kennington I enforced to about twenty thousand that great truth, "One thing is needful." Thence I went to Lambeth and showed (to the amazement, it seemed, of many who were present) how "he that is born of God does not commit sin" [1 John 3:9].

At eleven I preached at Bearfield to about three thousand, on the spirit of nature, of bondage, and of adoption.

Returning in the evening, I was exceedingly pressed to go back to a young woman in Kingswood. (The fact I nakedly relate and leave every man to his own judgment of it.) I went. She was nineteen or twenty years old, but, it seems, could not write or read. I found her on the bed, two or three persons holding her. It was a terrible sight. Anguish, horror, and despair above all description appeared in her pale face.

The thousand distortions of her whole body showed how the dogs of hell were gnawing her heart. The shrieks intermixed were scarcely to be endured. But her stony eyes could not weep. She screamed out, as soon as words could find their way, "I am damned, damned; lost forever! Six days ago you might have helped me. But it is past. I am the devil's now. I have given myself to him. His I am. Him I must serve. With him I must go to hell. His I am. Him I must serve. With him I must go to hell. I will be his. I will serve him. I will go with him to hell. I cannot be saved. I will not be saved. I must, I will, I will be damned!" She then began praying to the devil. We began: Arm of the Lord, awake, awake!

She immediately sank down as asleep; but, as soon as we left off, broke out again, with inexpressible vehemence: "Stony hearts, break! I am a warning to you. Break, break, poor stony hearts! I am damned that you may be saved. Now break, now break, poor stony hearts! You need not be damned, though I must." She then fixed her eyes on the corner of the ceiling and said: "There he is: ay, there he is! Come, good devil, come! Take me away. You said you would dash my brains out: come, do it quickly. I am yours. I will be yours. Come just now. Take me away."

What do you say to those who say that they don't mind going to Hell? Tell them to think about the power of God and the tiny "Hell's" of this life. God is the one who made the unbearable toothache that makes you want to scream, the headache that makes your head feel as though it could explode, the pain from a finger slammed in a car door, the agony of a hand that was burned on a toaster. He's the one who created you to panic in terror if you can't breathe. He holds your breath in His hands, and if he loses patience with you, He could simply stop your breathing and you would die in a moment and, if you die in your sins, you will find yourself damned. That means you will awake in Hell, in terrible agony with no way out.

God is to be feared, and it is His Word that promises "indignation and wrath, tribulation and anguish" (one up from pain) upon every soul that continues in evil. He will see that justice is done. He knows exactly how to punish evil to the full.

What do you say to those who say that they don't want to go to Heaven? Tell them to think about the power of God and the tiny "Heaven's" of this life. God is the one who created the breathtaking sunset, the beauty of a rose, the smile of a baby, the majesty of a lion, the sweet taste of an orange, and the wonderful intimacies of love.

If you die in your sins, you say goodbye forever to pleasure, and in its place you will receive pain and suffering for eternity.

If you die in Christ, you will say goodbye forever to pain and suffering, and in its place you will have unspeakable pleasure for eternity.

Behold the goodness and severity of God.—Ray Comfort

———•◦•———

We interrupted her by calling again upon God, on which she sank down as before; and another young woman began to roar out as loud as she had done. My brother now came in, it being about nine o'clock. We continued in prayer till past eleven, when God in a moment spoke peace into the soul, first of the first tormented, and then of the other. And they both joined in singing praise to Him who had "stilled the enemy and the avenger."

SATURDAY, 27 – I was sent forth to Kingswood again, to one of those who had been so ill before. A violent rain began just as I set out, so that I was thoroughly wet in a few minutes. Just at that time the woman (then three miles off) cried out, "Yonder comes Wesley, galloping as fast as he can." When I was come, I was quite cold and dead and fitter for sleep than prayer. She burst out into a horrid laughter and said, "No power, no power; no faith, no faith. She is mine; her soul is mine. I have her and will not let her go."

―――――・・―――――

This is the reality of demonic possession. For a similar encounter see, Out of the Comfort Zone *by Ray Comfort (Bridge Logos Publishers).*

―――――・・―――――

We begged of God to increase our faith. Meanwhile her pangs increased more and more so that one would have imagined, by the violence of the throes, her body must have been shattered to pieces. One who was clearly convinced this was no natural disorder said, "I think Satan is let loose. I fear he will not stop here." He added, "I command thee, in the name of the Lord Jesus, to tell if you have commission to torment any other soul." It was immediately answered, "I have. I—y C—r and S—h J—s." (two who lived at some distance, and were then in perfect health.)

We betook ourselves to prayer again and ceased not till she began, about six o'clock, with a clear voice and composed, cheerful look: Praise God, from whom all blessings flow.

Ibid, page 79, 81-82

"Though I am always in a haste," said Wesley, "I am never in a hurry, because I never undertake more work than I can go through with perfect calmness of spirit."

John Wesley the Methodist, The Methodist Book Concern, 1903

———•—•———

Everything we do as Christians should be done in a spirit of urgency, and everything we do for the Kingdom of God is of vital importance.—Ray Comfort

———•—•———

"As long as you feel your own weakness and helplessness, you will find help from above." Bonnie Sako, *Anthology of Religious Thought*, Allegheny Publications, 2001

———•—•———

Every now and then I have times when I have preached in the open air and the experience could only be described as nothing short of horrible. Most of the crowd dissipates as soon as I mention the things of God, and those who stay mock what little I feel I have to say. Although these occasional days are disheartening experiences, I can't but help but see them as important reminders that I can do nothing of myself-that without God's help I am weak and helpless. It is the horrible days that remind me that this work we call evangelism is His work in us, and without His help, nothing is accomplished. They drive us back to our knees in humbleness of heart, the place we should always be.—Ray Comfort

———•—•———

"Here then I am, far from the busy ways of men. I sit down alone; only God is here. In his presence I open, I read his Book; for this end, to find the way to heaven. Is there a doubt concerning the meaning of what I read? Does anything appear dark or intricate? I lift up my heart to the Father of lights: 'Lord, is it not your Word, "If any man lack wisdom, let him ask of God"? You "give liberally and upbraid not." You have said, "If any be willing to do thy will, he shall know." I am willing to do, let me know thy will.' I then search after and consider parallel passages of Scripture, 'comparing spiritual things with spiritual'. I meditate thereon, with all the attention and earnestness of which my mind is capable. If any doubt still remains, I consult those who are experienced in the things of God, and then the writings whereby, being dead, they yet speak. And what I thus learn, that I teach." [John Wesley, *Preface to Standard Sermons*].

"God himself has condescended to teach the way: for this very end He came from heaven. He has written it down in a book. O give me that book! At any price give me the Book of God!" [John Wesley, *Preface to Standard Sermons*].

How many Bibles do you own? If you live in the United Sates, you probably own more than one. Abundance can make us take God's Word for granted. Do you read His Word every day, without fail. You should, if you love Him. Do you feed your belly every day? Which comes first in your life—your Bible or your belly?—Ray Comfort

---

"Nay, if there be any mistakes in the Bible, there may as well be a thousand. If there be one falsehood in that book, it did not come from the God of truth" (John Wesley, Journal, 24 July 1776).

All Scripture is given by inspiration from God Himself. Any mistakes we find are our mistakes.—Ray Comfort

———•◦•———

"Nay, will not the allowing there is any error in Scripture, shake the authority of the whole?" (*Works*, Jackson ed., 9:150).

———•◦•———

This kind of faith in God is rare in an age where many accept "scribal errors."—Ray Comfort

———•◦•———

"The faith of the Protestants, in general, embraces only those truths, as necessary to salvation, which are clearly revealed in the oracles of God. Whatever is plainly declared in the Old and New Testaments is the object of their faith. They believe neither more nor less than what is manifestly contained in, and provable by, the Holy Scriptures ... The written Word is the whole and sole rule of their faith, as well as practice. They believe whatsoever God has declared, and profess to do whatsoever He hath commanded. This is the proper faith of Protestants: by this they will abide, and no other." [John Wesley, "On Faith," Sermon #106, I.8].

"Try all things by the written Word, and let all bow down before it. You are in danger of [fanaticism] every hour, if you depart ever so little from Scripture; yea, or from the plain, literal meaning of an text, taken in connection with the context." (*Works*, 11:429).

"It would be excusable if these menders of the Bible would offer their hypotheses modestly. But one cannot excuse them when they not only obtrude their novel scheme, with the utmost confidence, but even ridicule that scriptural one which always was and is now held by men of the greatest learning and piety in the world. Hereby they promote the cause of infidelity more effectually than either Hume or Voltaire." (Wesley's Journal, 8 August 1773).

Wesley's advice on teaching. "1. To invite. 2. To convince. 3. To offer Christ. 4. To build up. And to do this in some measure in every sermon." John Wesley the Methodist, The Methodist Booked Concern, 1903

Wesley, John, 1703–91, English evangelical preacher, founder of Methodism, B. Epworth, Lincolnshire.

His Early Life

Wesley was ordained a deacon in the Church of England in 1725, elected a fellow of Lincoln College, Oxford, in 1726, and ordained a priest in 1728. At Oxford he took the lead (1729) in a group of students that included his younger brother, Charles Wesley, and George Whitefield. They were derisively called "methodists" for their methodical devotion to study and religious duties.

In 1735, the Wesleys accompanied James Oglethorpe to Georgia, John to serve there as a missionary and Charles to act as secretary to Oglethorpe. During John Wesley's two-year stay in the colony he was deeply influenced by Moravian missionaries; upon his return to England he made many Moravian friends. On May 24, 1738, at a meeting of a small religious society in Aldersgate St., London, Wesley experienced a religious conversion while listening to a reading of Martin Luther's preface to the Epistle to the Romans. This experience of salvation through faith in Christ alone was the burden of his message for the rest of his life.

— • —

When I discovered this, I was immediately curious as to what Wesley read that so touched his heart (he later wrote that while reading it "I felt my heart strangely warmed"). You may also be curious, so here, in its entirety, is Martin Luther's Preface to the Letter of St. Paul to the Romans]:

This letter is truly the most important piece in the New Testament. It is purest Gospel. It is well worth a Christian's while not only to memorize it word for word but also to occupy himself with it daily, as though it were the daily bread of the soul. It is impossible to read or to meditate on this letter too much or too well. The more one deals with it, the more precious it becomes and the better it tastes.

Therefore I want to carry out my service and, with this preface, provide an introduction to the letter, insofar as God gives me the ability, so that every one can gain the fullest possible understanding of it. Up to now it has been darkened by glosses [explanatory notes and comments which accompany a text] and by many a useless comment, but it is in itself a bright light, almost bright enough to illumine the entire Scripture.

To begin with, we have to become familiar with the vocabulary of the letter and know what St. Paul means by the words law, sin, grace, faith, justice, flesh, spirit, etc. Otherwise there is no use in reading it.

You must not understand the word law here in human fashion, i.e., a regulation about what sort of works must be done or must not be done. That's the way it is with human laws: you satisfy the demands of the law with works, whether your heart is in it or not. God judges what is in the depths of the heart. Therefore his law also makes demands on the depths of the heart and doesn't let the heart rest content in works; rather it punishes as hypocrisy and lies all works done apart from the depths of the heart. All human beings are called liars (Psalm 116), since none of them keeps or can keep God's law from the depths of the heart. Everyone finds inside himself an aversion to good and a craving for evil. Where there is no free desire for good, there the heart has not set itself on God's law. There also sin is surely to be found and the deserved wrath of God, whether a lot of good works and an honorable life appear outwardly or not.

Therefore in chapter 2, St. Paul adds that the Jews are all sinners and says that only the doers of the law are justified in the sight of God. What he is saying is that no one is a doer of the law by works. On the contrary, he says to them, "You teach that one should not commit adultery, and you commit adultery. You judge another in a certain matter and condemn yourselves in that same matter, because you do the very same thing that you judged in another." It is as if he were saying, "Outwardly you live quite properly in the works of the law and judge those who do not live the same way; you know how to teach everybody. You see the speck in another's eye but do not notice the beam in your own."

Outwardly you keep the law with works out of fear of punishment or love of gain. Likewise you do everything without free desire and love of the law; you act out of aversion and force. You'd rather act otherwise if the law didn't exist. It follows then that you, in the depths of your heart, are an enemy of the law. What do you mean, therefore, by teaching another not to steal, when you, in the depths of your heart, are a thief and would be one outwardly too if you dared. (Of course, outward work doesn't last long with such hypocrites.) So then, you teach others but not yourself; you don't even know what you are teaching. You've never understood the law rightly. Furthermore, the law increases sin, as St. Paul says in chapter 5. That is because a person becomes more and more an enemy of the law the more it demands of him what he can't possibly do.

In chapter 7, St. Paul says, "The law is spiritual." What does that mean? If the law were physical, then it could be satisfied by works; but since it is spiritual, no one can satisfy it unless everything he does springs from the depths of the heart. But no one can give such a heart except the Spirit of God, who makes the person to be like the law, so that he actually conceives a heartfelt longing for the law and henceforward does everything, not through fear or coercion, but from a free heart. Such a law is spiritual since it can only be loved and fulfilled by such a heart and such a spirit. If the Spirit is not in the heart, then there remain sin, aversion and enmity against the law, which in itself is good, just and holy.

You must get used to the idea that it is one thing to do the works of the law and quite another to fulfill it. The works of the law are every thing that a person does or can do of his own free will and by his own powers in order to obey the law. But because in doing such works the heart abhors the law and yet is forced to obey it, the works are a total loss and are completely useless. That is what St. Paul means in chapter 3 when he says, "No human being is justified before God through the works of the law." From this you can see that the schoolmasters [i.e., the scholastic theologians] and sophists are seducers when they teach that you can prepare yourself for grace by means of works. How can anybody prepare himself for good by means of works if he does no good work except with aversion and constraint in his heart? How can such a work please God, if it proceeds from an averse and unwilling heart?

But to fulfill the law means to do its work eagerly, lovingly and freely, without the constraint of the law; it means to live well and in a manner pleasing to God, as though there were no law or punishment. It is the Holy Spirit, however, who puts such eagerness of unconstrained love into the heart, as Paul says in chapter 5. But the Spirit is given only in, with, and through faith in Jesus Christ, as Paul says in his introduction. So also, faith comes only through the word of God, the Gospel, that preaches Christ: how he is both Son of God and man, how he died and rose for our sake. Paul says all this in chapters 3, 4 and 10.

That is why faith alone makes someone just and fulfills the law; faith it is that brings the Holy Spirit through the merits of Christ. The Spirit, in turn, renders the heart glad and free, as the law demands. Then good works proceed from faith itself. That is what Paul means in chapter 3 when, after he has thrown out the works of the law, he sounds as though he wants to abolish the law by faith. No, he says, we uphold the law through faith; i.e., we fulfill it through faith.

Sin in the Scriptures means not only external works of the body but also all those movements within us which bestir themselves and move us to do the external works, namely, the depth of the heart with all its powers. Therefore the word do should refer to a person's completely falling into sin. No external work of sin happens, after all, unless a person commits himself to it completely, body and soul. In particular, the Scriptures see into the heart, to the root and main source of all sin: unbelief in the depth of the heart. Thus, even as faith alone makes just and brings the Spirit and the desire to do good external works, so it is only unbelief which sins and exalts the flesh and brings desire to do evil external works. That's what happened to Adam and Eve in Paradise (cf. Genesis 3).

That is why only unbelief is called sin by Christ, as he says in John, chapter 16 (v.9), "The Spirit will punish the world because of sin, because it does not believe in me." Furthermore, before good or bad works happen, which are the good or bad fruits of the heart, there has to be present in the heart either faith or unbelief—the root, sap and chief power of all sin. That is why, in the Scriptures, unbelief is called the head of the serpent and of the ancient dragon which the offspring of the woman, i.e., Christ, must crush, as was promised to Adam (cf. Genesis 3). Grace and gift differ in that grace actually denotes God's kindness or favor which he has toward us and by which he is disposed to pour Christ and the Spirit with his gifts into us, as becomes clear from chapter 5, where Paul says, "Grace and gift are in Christ, etc." The gifts and the Spirit increase daily in us, yet they are not complete, since evil desires and sins remain in us which war against the Spirit, as Paul says in chapter 7, and in Galatians chapter 5. And Genesis chapter 3 proclaims the enmity between the offspring of the woman and that of the serpent. But grace does do this much: we are accounted completely just before God. God's grace is not divided into bits and pieces, as are the gifts, but grace takes us up completely into God's favor for the sake of Christ, our intercessor and mediator, so that the gifts may begin their work in us.

In this way, then, you should understand chapter 7, where St. Paul portrays himself as still a sinner, while in chapter 8 he says that, because of the incomplete gifts and because of the Spirit, there is nothing damnable in those who are in Christ. Because our flesh has not been killed, we are still sinners, but because we believe in Christ and have the beginnings of the Spirit, God so shows us his favor and mercy, that he neither notices nor judges such sins. Rather he deals with us according to our belief in Christ until sin is killed.

Faith is not that human illusion and dream that some people think it is. When they hear and talk a lot about faith and yet see that no moral improvement and no good works result from it, they fall into error and say, "Faith is not enough. You must do works if you want to be virtuous and get to heaven." The result is that, when they hear the Gospel, they stumble and make for themselves with their own powers a concept in their hearts which says, "I believe." This concept they hold to be true faith. But since it is a human fabrication and thought, and not an experience of the heart, it accomplishes nothing, and there follows no improvement.

Faith is a work of God in us, which changes us and brings us to birth anew from God (cf. John 1). It kills the old Adam, makes us completely different people in heart, mind, senses, and all our powers, and brings the Holy Spirit with it. What a living, creative, active powerful thing is faith! It is impossible that faith ever stops doing good. Faith doesn't ask whether good works are to be done, but, before it is asked, it has done them. It is always active. Whoever doesn't do such works is without faith; he gropes and searches about him for faith and good works but doesn't know what faith or good works are. Even so, he chatters on with a great many words about faith and good works.

Faith is a living, unshakeable confidence in God's grace; it is so certain that someone would die a thousand times for it. This kind of trust in and knowledge of God's grace makes a person joyful, confident, and happy with regard to God and all creatures. This is what the Holy Spirit does by faith. Through faith, a person will do good to everyone without coercion, willingly and happily; he will serve everyone and suffer everything for the love and praise of God, who has shown him such grace. It is as impossible to separate works from faith as burning and shining from fire. Therefore be on guard against your own false ideas and against the chatterers who think they are clever enough to make judgments about faith and good works but who are in reality the biggest fools. Ask God to work faith in you; otherwise you will remain eternally without faith, no matter what you try to do or fabricate.

Now justice is just such a faith. It is called God's justice or that justice which is valid in God's sight, because it is God who gives it and reckons it as justice for the sake of Christ our Mediator. It influences a person to give to everyone what he owes him. Through faith a person becomes sinless and eager for God's commands. Thus he gives God the honor due him and pays him what he owes him. He serves people willingly with the means available to him. In this way he pays everyone his due. Neither nature nor free will nor our own powers can bring about such a justice, for even as no one can give himself faith, so too he cannot remove unbelief. How then can he take away even the smallest sin? Therefore everything which takes place outside faith or in unbelief is lie, hypocrisy and sin (Romans 14), no matter how smoothly it may seem to go.

You must not understand flesh here as denoting only unchastity or spirit as denoting only the inner heart. Here St. Paul calls flesh (as does Christ in John 3) everything born of flesh; i.e., the whole human being with body and soul, reason and senses, since everything in him tends toward the flesh. That is why you should know enough to call that person "fleshly" who, without grace, fabricates, teaches and chatters about high spiritual matters. You can learn the same thing from Galatians chapter 5, where St. Paul calls heresy and hatred works of the flesh. And in Romans chapter 8, he says that through the flesh the law is weakened. He says this, not of unchastity, but of all sins, most of all of unbelief, which is the most spiritual of vices.

On the other hand, you should know enough to call that person "spiritual" who is occupied with the most outward of works as was Christ, when he washed the feet of the disciples; and Peter, when he steered his boat and fished. So then, a person is "flesh" who, inwardly and outwardly, lives only to do those things which are of use to the flesh and to temporal existence. A person is "spirit" who, inwardly and outwardly, lives only to do those things which are of use to the spirit and to the life to come.

Unless you understand these words in this way, you will never understand either this letter of St. Paul or any book of the Scriptures. Be on guard therefore against any teacher who uses these words differently, no matter who he be, whether Jerome, Augustine, Ambrose, Origen or anyone else as great as or greater than they. Now let us turn to the letter itself.

The first duty of a preacher of the Gospel is, through his revealing of the law and of sin, to rebuke and to turn into sin everything in life that does not have the Spirit and faith in Christ as its base. [Here and elsewhere in Luther's preface, as indeed in Romans itself, it is not clear whether "spirit" has the meaning "Holy Spirit" or "spiritual person," as Luther has previously defined it.] Thereby he will lead people to a recognition of their miserable condition, and thus they will become humble and yearn for help. This is what St. Paul does. He begins in chapter 1 by rebuking the gross sins and unbelief which are in plain view, as were (and still are) the sins of the pagans, who live without God's grace. He says that, through the Gospel, God is revealing his wrath from heaven upon all mankind because of the godless and unjust lives they live. For, although they know and recognize day by day that there is a God, yet human nature in itself, without grace, is so evil that it neither thanks nor honors God. This nature blinds itself and continually falls into wickedness, even going so far as to commit idolatry and other horrible sins and vices. It is unashamed of itself and leaves such things unpunished in others.

In chapter 2, St. Paul extends his rebuke to those who appear outwardly pious or who sin secretly. Such were the Jews, and such are all hypocrites still, who live virtuous lives but without eagerness and love; in their heart they are enemies of God's law and like to judge other people. That's the way with hypocrites: they think that they are pure but are actually full of greed, hate, pride and all sorts of filth (cf. Matthew 23). These are they who despise God's goodness and, by their hardness of heart, heap wrath upon themselves. Thus Paul explains the law rightly when he lets no one remain without sin but proclaims the wrath of God to all who want to live virtuously by nature or by free will. He makes them out to be no better than public sinners; he says they are hard of heart and unrepentant.

In chapter 3, Paul lumps both secret and public sinners together: the one, he says, is like the other; all are sinners in the sight of God. Besides, the Jews had God's word, even though many did not believe in it. But still God's truth and faith in him are not thereby rendered useless. St. Paul introduces, as an aside, the saying from Psalm 51, that God remains true to his words. Then he returns to his topic and proves from Scripture that they are all sinners and that no one becomes just through the works of the law, but that God gave the law only so that sin might be perceived.

Next St. Paul teaches the right way to be virtuous and to be saved; he says that they are all sinners, unable to glory in God. They must, however, be justified through faith in Christ, who has merited this for us by his blood and has become for us a mercy seat [cf. Exodus 25:17, Leviticus

16:14ff, and John 2:2] in the presence of God, who forgives us all our previous sins. In so doing, God proves that it is his justice alone, which he gives through faith, that helps us—the justice which was at the appointed time revealed through the Gospel and, previous to that, was witnessed to by the Law and the Prophets. Therefore the law is set up by faith, but the works of the law, along with the glory taken in them, are knocked down by faith. [As with the term "spirit," the word "law" seems to have for Luther, and for St. Paul, two meanings. Sometimes it means "regulation about what must be done or not done," as in the third paragraph of this preface; sometimes it means "the Torah," as in the previous sentence. And sometimes it seems to have both meanings, as in what follows.]

In chapters 1 to 3, St. Paul has revealed sin for what it is and has taught the way of faith which leads to justice. Now in chapter 4 he deals with some objections and criticisms. He takes up first the one that people raise who, on hearing that faith makes just without works, say, "What? Shouldn't we do any good works?" Here St. Paul holds up Abraham as an example. He says, "What did Abraham accomplish with his good works? Were they all good for nothing and useless?" He concludes that Abraham was made righteous apart from all his works by faith alone. Even before the "work" of his circumcision, Scripture praises him as being just on account of faith alone (cf. Genesis 15). Now if the work of his circumcision did nothing to make him just, a work that God had commanded him to do and hence a work of obedience, then surely no other good work can do anything to make a person just. Even as Abraham's circumcision was an outward sign with which he proved his justice based on faith, so too all good works are only outward signs which flow from faith and are the fruits of faith; they prove that the person is already inwardly just in the sight of God.

St. Paul verifies his teaching on faith in chapter 3 with a powerful example from Scripture. He calls as a witness David, who says in Psalm 32 that a person becomes just without works but doesn't remain without works once he has become just. Then Paul extends this example and applies it against all other works of the law. He concludes that the Jews cannot be Abraham's heirs just because of their blood relationship to him and still less because of the works of the law. Rather, they have to inherit Abraham's faith if they want to be his real heirs, since it was prior to the Law of Moses and the law of circumcision that Abraham became just through faith and was called a father of all believers. St. Paul adds that the law brings about more wrath than grace, because no one obeys it with love and eagerness. More disgrace than grace comes from the works of the law. Therefore faith alone can obtain the grace promised to Abraham. Examples like these are written for our sake, that we also should have faith.

In chapter 5, St. Paul comes to the fruits and works of faith, namely: joy, peace, love for God and for all people; in addition: assurance, steadfastness, confidence, courage, and hope in sorrow and suffering. All of these follow where faith is genuine, because of the overflowing goodwill that God has shown in Christ: he had him die for us before we could ask him for it, yes, even while we were still his enemies. Thus we have established that faith, without any good works, makes just. It does not follow from that, however, that we should not do good works; rather it means that morally upright works do not remain lacking. About such works the "works-holy" people know nothing; they invent for themselves their own works in which are neither peace nor joy nor assurance nor love nor hope nor steadfastness nor any kind of genuine Christian works or faith.

Next St. Paul makes a digression, a pleasant little side-trip, and relates where both sin and justice, death and life come *from. He opposes these two: Adam and Christ. What he wants to say is that Christ, a second Adam, had to come in order to make us heirs of his justice through a new spiritual birth in faith, just as the old Adam made us heirs of sin through the old fleshy birth.*

St. Paul proves, by this reasoning, that a person cannot help himself by his works to get from sin to justice any more than he can prevent his own physical birth. St. Paul also proves that the divine law, which should have been well-suited, if anything was, for helping people to obtain justice, not only was no help at all when it did come, but it even increased sin. Evil human nature, consequently, becomes more hostile to it; the more the law forbids it to indulge its own desires, the more it wants to. Thus the law makes Christ all the more necessary and demands more grace to help human nature. In chapter 6, St. Paul takes up the special work of faith, the struggle which the spirit wages against the flesh to kill off those sins and desires that remain after a person has been made just. He teaches us that faith doesn't so free us from sin that we can be idle, lazy and self-assured, as though there were no more sin in us. Sin is there, but because of faith that struggles against it, God does not reckon sin as deserving damnation. Therefore we have in our own selves a lifetime of work cut out for us; we have to tame our body, kill its lusts, and force its members to obey the spirit and not the lusts. We must do this so that we may conform to the death and resurrection of Christ and complete our Baptism, which signifies a death to sin and a new life of grace. Our aim is to be completely clean from sin and then to rise bodily with Christ and live forever.

St. Paul says that we can accomplish all this because we are in grace and not in the law. He explains that to be "outside the law" is not the same as having no law and being able to do what you please. No, being "under the law" means living without grace, surrounded by the works of the law.

Then surely sin reigns by means of the law, since no one is naturally well-disposed toward the law. That very condition, however, is the greatest sin. But grace makes the law lovable to us, so there is then no sin any more, and the law is no longer against us but one with us.

This is true freedom from sin and from the law; St. Paul writes about this for the rest of the chapter. He says it is a freedom only to do good with eagerness and to live a good life without the coercion of the law. This freedom is, therefore, a spiritual freedom which does not suspend the law but which supplies what the law demands, namely eagerness and love. These silence the law so that it has no further cause to drive people on and make demands of them. It's as though you owed something to a moneylender and couldn't pay him. You could be rid of him in one of two ways: either he would take nothing from you and would tear up his account book, or a pious man would pay for you and give you what you needed to satisfy your debt. That's exactly how Christ freed us from the law. Therefore our freedom is not a wild, fleshy freedom that has no obligation to do anything. On the contrary, it is a freedom that does a great deal, indeed everything, yet is free of the law's demands and debts.

In chapter 7, St. Paul confirms the foregoing by an analogy drawn from married life. When a man dies, the wife is free; the one is free and clear of the other. It is not the case that the woman may not or should not marry another man; rather she is now for the first time free to marry someone else. She could not do this before she was free of her first husband. In the same way, our conscience is bound to the law so long as our condition is that of the sinful old man. But when the old man is killed by the spirit, then the conscience is free, and conscience and law are quit of each other. Not that conscience should now do nothing; rather, it should now for the first time truly cling to its second husband, Christ, and bring forth the fruit of life.

Next, St. Paul sketches further the nature of sin and the law. It is the law that makes sin really active and powerful, because the old man gets more and more hostile to the law since he can't pay the debt demanded by the law. Sin is his very nature; of himself he can't do otherwise. And so the law is his death and torture. Now the law is not itself evil; it is our evil nature that cannot tolerate that the good law should demand good from it. It's like the case of a sick person, who cannot tolerate that you demand that he run and jump around and do other things that a healthy person does.

St. Paul concludes here that if we understand the law properly and comprehend it in the best possible way, then we will see that its sole function is to remind us of our sins, to kill us by our sins, and to make us deserving of eternal wrath. Conscience learns and experiences all this in detail when it comes face-to- face with the law. It follows then that we must have something else over and above the law which can make a person virtuous and cause him to be saved. Those, however, who do not understand the law rightly are blind; they go their way boldly and think they are satisfying the law with works. They don't know how much the law demands, namely, a free, willing, eager heart. That is the reason that they don't see Moses rightly before their eyes. [In both Jewish and Christian teaching, Moses was commonly held to be the author of the Pentateuch, the first five books of the Bible. Cf. the involved imagery of Moses' face and the veil over it in 2 Corinthians 3:7–18.] For them he is covered and concealed by the veil.

Then St. Paul shows how spirit and flesh struggle with each other in one person. He gives himself as an example, so that we may learn how to kill sin in ourselves. He gives both spirit and flesh the name "law," so that, just as it is in the nature of divine law to drive a person on and make demands of him, so too the flesh drives and demands and rages against the spirit and wants to have its own way. Likewise the spirit drives and demands against the flesh and wants to have its own way. This feud lasts in us for as long as we live, in one person more, in another less, depending on whether spirit or flesh is stronger. Yet the whole human being is both spirit and flesh. The human being fights with himself until he becomes completely spiritual.

In chapter 8, St. Paul comforts fighters such as these and tells them that this flesh will not bring them condemnation. He goes on to show what the nature of flesh and spirit are. Spirit, he says, comes from Christ, who has given us his Holy Spirit; the Holy Spirit makes us spiritual and restrains the flesh. The Holy Spirit assures us that we are God's children no matter how furiously sin may rage within us, so long as we follow the Spirit and struggle against sin in order to kill it. Because nothing is so effective in deadening the flesh as the cross and suffering, Paul comforts us in our suffering. He says that the Spirit, [cf. previous note about the meaning of "spirit."] love and all creatures will stand by us; the Spirit in us groans and all creatures long with us that we be freed from the flesh and from sin. Thus we see that these three chapters—6, 7 and 8—all deal with the one work of faith, which is to kill the old Adam and to constrain the flesh.

In chapters 9, 10 and 11, St. Paul teaches us about the eternal providence of God. It is the original source which determines who would believe and who wouldn't, who can be set free from sin and who cannot. Such matters have been taken out of our hands and are put into God's hands so that we might become virtuous. It is absolutely necessary that it be so, for we are so weak and unsure of ourselves that if it depended on us no human being would be saved. The devil would overpower all of us. But God is steadfast;

his providence will not fail, and no one can prevent its realization. Therefore we have hope against sin.

But here we must shut the mouths of those sacrilegious and arrogant spirits who, mere beginners that they are, bring their reason to bear on this matter; and commence, from their exalted position, to probe the abyss of divine providence and uselessly trouble themselves about whether they are predestined or not. These people must surely plunge to their ruin, since they will either despair or abandon themselves to a life of chance.

You, however, follow the reasoning of this letter in the order in which it is presented. Fix your attention first of all on Christ and the Gospel, so that you may recognize your sin and his grace. Then struggle against sin, as chapters 1-8 have taught you to. Finally, when you have come, in chapter 8, under the shadow of the cross and suffering, they will teach you, in chapters 9–11, about providence and what a comfort it is. [The context here and in St. Paul's letter makes it clear that this is the cross and passion, not only of Christ, but of each Christian.] Apart from suffering, the cross and the pangs of death, you cannot come to grips with providence without harm to yourself and secret anger against God. The old Adam must be quite dead before you can endure this matter and drink this strong wine. Therefore make sure you don't drink wine while you are still a babe at the breast. There is a proper measure, time and age for understanding every doctrine.

In chapter 12, St. Paul teaches the true liturgy and makes all Christians priests, so that they may offer, not money or cattle, as priests do in the Law, but their own bodies, by putting their desires to death. Next he describes the outward conduct of Christians whose lives are governed by the Spirit; he tells how they teach, preach, rule, serve, give, suffer, love, live and act toward friend, foe and everyone.

These are the works that a Christian does, for, as I have said, faith is not idle.

In chapter 13, St. Paul teaches that one should honor and obey the secular authorities. He includes this, not because it makes people virtuous in the sight of God, but because it does insure that the virtuous have outward peace and protection and that the wicked cannot do evil without fear and in undisturbed peace. Therefore it is the duty of virtuous people to honor secular authority, even though they do not, strictly speaking, need it. Finally, St. Paul sums up everything in love and gathers it all into the example of Christ: what he has done for us, we must also do and follow after him.

In chapter 14, St. Paul teaches that one should carefully guide those with weak conscience and spare them. One shouldn't use Christian freedom to harm, but rather to help the weak. Where that isn't done, there follow dissension and despising of the Gospel, on which everything else depends. It is better to give way a little to the weak in faith until they become stronger than to have the teaching of the Gospel perish completely. This work is a particularly necessary work of love, especially now when people, by eating meat and by other freedoms, are brashly, boldly and unnecessarily shaking weak consciences which have not yet come to know the truth.

In chapter 15, St. Paul cites Christ as an example to show that we must also have patience with the weak, even those who fail by sinning publicly or by their disgusting morals. We must not cast them aside but must bear with them until they become better. That is the way Christ treated us and still treats us every day; he puts up with our vices, our wicked morals and all our imperfection, and he helps us ceaselessly. Finally Paul prays for the Christians at Rome; he praises them and commends them to God. He points out his own office and the message that he preaches. He makes an unobtrusive plea for a contribution for the poor in Jerusalem. Unalloyed love is the basis of all he says and does.

The last chapter consists of greetings. But Paul also includes a salutary warning against human doctrines which are preached alongside the Gospel and which do a great deal of harm. It's as though he had clearly seen that out of Rome and through the Romans would come the deceitful, harmful Canons and Decretals along with the entire brood and swarm of human laws and commands that is now drowning the whole world and has blotted out this letter and the whole of the Scriptures, along with the Spirit and faith. Nothing remains but the idol Belly, and St. Paul depicts those people here as its servants. God deliver us from them. Amen.

We find in this letter, then, the richest possible teaching about what a Christian should know: the meaning of law, Gospel, sin, punishment, grace, faith, justice, Christ, God, good works, love, hope and the cross. We learn how we are to act toward everyone, toward the virtuous and sinful, toward the strong and the weak, friend and foe, and toward ourselves. Paul bases everything firmly on Scripture and proves his points with examples from his own experience and from the Prophets, so that nothing more could be desired. Therefore it seems that St. Paul, in writing this letter, wanted to compose a summary of the whole of Christian and evangelical teaching which would also be an introduction to the whole Old Testament. Without doubt, whoever takes this letter to heart possesses the light and power of the Old Testament. Therefore each and every Christian should make this letter the habitual and constant object of his study. God grant us his grace to do so. Amen.—Ray Comfort

---

This translation was made by Andrew Thornton, OSB, for the Saint Anselm College Humanities Program, 1983 by Saint Anselm Abbey.

Two Questions

To his young men returning from preaching Wesley asked two questions. Did anyone get saved? Did anyone get mad? If they answered no to both he told them they were not called to preach for a sermon will either lead a soul to Christ or the truth will anger them.

Wesley Quotes

As to things which do not strike at the root of Christianity, we think and let think."

"You have nothing to do but to save souls; therefore spend and be spent in this work."

"As long as you feel your own weakness and helplessness, you will always find help from above."

"The longer I live, the larger allowances I make for human infirmities. I exact more from myself and less from others."

Who would not rather be on the footing he is now—under a covenant of mercy? Who would wish to hazard a whole eternity upon one mistake? Is it not infinitely more desirable to be in a state wherein, though encompassed with infirmities, yet we do not run such a desperate risk, but if we fall, we may rise again, wherein we may say:

My trespass is grown up to heaven; but far above the skies/ in Christ abundantly forgiven, I see thy mercies rise!

[Prior to Aldersgate] "I went to America to convert the Indians, but oh, who shall convert me? ... I went to America to convert others, [but] was never myself converted to God."

[Also prior to Aldersgate] "All this time I conversed much with Peter Bohler; but I understood him not, and least of all when he said, 'My brother, my brother, that philosophy of yours must be purged away'... it struck into my mind, 'Leave off preaching. How can you preach to others who have not faith yourself?' I asked Bohler whether I should leave off or not. He answered, 'By no means ... Preach faith till you have it; and then, because you have it, you will preach faith.'"

[Of Aldersgate] "What occurred on Wednesday the 24th I think best to relate at large ... In the evening I went very unwillingly to a society in Aldersgate Street, where one was reading Luther's preface to the Epistle to the Romans. About a quarter to nine, while he was describing the change which God works in the heart through faith in Christ, I felt my heart strangely warmed. I felt I did trust in Christ, Christ alone *for salvation;* and an assurance was given me that He had taken away my sins, even mine, and saved me from the law of sin and death."

The Methodists must take heed to their doctrine, their experience, their practice, and their discipline. If they attend to their doctrines only, they will make the people antinomians; if to the experimental part of religion only, they will make them enthusiasts; if to the practical part only, they will make them Pharisees; and if they do not attend to their discipline, they will be like persons who bestow much pains in cultivating their garden, and put no fence round it, to save it from the wild boar of the forest.

"God loves you; therefore love and obey him. Christ died for you; therefore die to sin. Christ is risen; therefore rise in the image of God. Christ liveth ever more; therefore live to God till you live with him in glory. So we preached; and so you believed! This is the scriptural way, the Methodist way, the true way. God grant that we may never turn therefrom, to the right hand or to the left."

The Law

To slay the sinner is, then, the First use of the law; to destroy the life and strength wherein he trusts, and convince him that he is dead while he lives; not only under the sentence of death, but actually dead unto God, void of all spiritual life, 'dead in trespasses and sins.' The Second use of it is to bring him unto life, unto Christ, that he may live. It is true, in performing both these offices, it acts the part of a severe schoolmaster. It drives us by force, rather than draws us by love. And yet love is the spring of all. It is the spirit of love which, by this painful means, tears away our confidence in the flesh, which leaves us no broken reed whereon to trust, and so constrains the sinner, stripped of all, to cry out in the bitterness of his soul, or groan in the depth of his heart, 'I give up every plea beside, – Lord, I am damn'd; but Thou hast died.'"

John Wesley, Sermon, The Original, Nature, Property, and Use of Law (The Sermons of John Wesley 1872 Edition) (Thomas Jackson, editor)

This is such a profound and wonderful statement. It draws us by force, and yet it is love that motivates those who use the Law and Him who provide the Law. Its purpose is to drive us to salvation is Christ, not damnation in Hell. Never take it to heart when someone accuses you of being unloving, because you use the Law as a schoolmaster to bring sinners to Christ.—Ray Comfort

Evangelistic Responsibility

You have nothing to do but to save souls. Therefore spend and be spent in this work. And go not only to those that need you, but to those that need you most ... It is not your business to preach so many times, and to take care of this or that society; but to save as many souls as you can; to bring as many sinners as you possibly can to repentance."

Nothing else matters. Love for the lost is all-consuming. The firefighter who climbs the ladder to reach a mother and child trapped on the ledge of a burning building will focus on one thing alone—deliverance for those in danger.—Ray Comfort

"Give me one hundred men who fear nothing but sin and desire nothing but God, and I care not whether they be clergyman or laymen, they alone will shake the gates of Hell and set up the kingdom of Heaven upon the earth."

In March of 2007, there was a tragic fire in a convalescent home in East Russia. Sixty-two elderly people died, because the watchman ignored two alarms. He didn't do anything until he saw the flames. The town decided a year earlier that it couldn't afford a fire department. Sixty-two precious lives were lost—grandmothers and grandfathers, moms and dads … they said they couldn't afford it, and look at what it cost them.

The contemporary church is like that town. Bill Bright said that only 2% of the Church in America regularly shares their faith with others. The Church doesn't give evangelism priority. Ever since I came to live in the United States I have been fascinated by what happens on the roads when an emergency vehicle wants to get through. Everything stops. Drivers pull over to the side of the road to give it free course. The law says that they must be given priority because someone's life may be at stake.

That's what the Church must do when it comes to evangelism. Everything else should stop to let it through. Evangelism must have priority because people's lives—their eternal salvation, is at stake. Let's not be like the watchman. Let's not wait until we see the flames before we sound the alarm.—Ray Comfort

The Noisy Mob

SUNDAY, SEPTEMBER 14 (London) – As I returned home in the evening, I had no sooner stepped out of the coach than the mob, who were gathered in great numbers about my door, quite closed me in. I rejoiced and blessed God, knowing this was the time I had long been looking for, and immediately spoke to those that were next me of "righteousness, and judgment to come." At first not many heard, the noise round about us being exceedingly great. But the silence spread farther and farther till I had a quiet, attentive congregation; and when I left them, they all showed much love and dismissed me with many blessings.

In Season, Out of Season

FRIDAY, 8 – I found myself much out of order. However, I made shift to preach in the evening; but on Saturday my bodily strength quite failed so that for several hours I could scarcely lift up my head. Sunday, 10. I was obliged to lie down most part of the day, being easy only in that posture. Yet in the evening my weakness was suspended while I was calling sinners to repentance. But at our love-feast which followed, beside the pain in my back and head and the fever which still continued upon me, just as I began to pray I was seized with such a cough that I could hardly speak. At the same time came strongly into my mind, "These signs shall follow them that believe" [Mark 16:17]. I called on Jesus aloud to "increase my faith" and to "confirm the word of his grace." While I was speaking, my pain vanished away; the fever left me; my bodily strength returned; and for many weeks I felt neither weakness nor pain. "Unto thee, O Lord, do I give thanks."

"Herald and preach the Word! Keep your sense of urgency [stand by, be at hand and ready], whether the opportunity seems to be favorable or unfavorable. [Whether it is convenient or inconvenient, whether it is welcome or unwelcome, you as preacher of the Word are to show people in what way their lives are wrong.] And convince them, rebuking and correcting, warning and urging and encouraging them, being unflagging and inexhaustible in patience and teaching." 2 Timothy 4:2 (Amplified Bible)—
Ray Comfort

The Experiment

MONDAY, JUNE 8 – I set out from Enfield Chace for Leicestershire. In the evening we came to Northampton, and the next afternoon to Mr. Ellis's at Markfield, five or six miles beyond Leicester. For these two days I had made an experiment which I had been so often and earnestly pressed to do—speaking to none concerning the things of God unless my heart was free to it. And what was the event? Why, 1.) that I spoke to none at all for fourscore miles together; no, not even to him that traveled with me in the chaise, unless a few words at first setting out; 2.) That I had no cross either to bear or to take up, and commonly, in an hour or two, fell fast asleep; 3.) That I had much respect shown me wherever I came, everyone behaving to me as to a civil, good-natured gentleman. Oh, how pleasing is all this to flesh and blood! Need ye "compass sea and land" to make "proselytes" to this?

The flesh, the world and the devil love it when you stop sharing your faith.—Ray Comfort

Immediate Conversation

Monday, 17 – I had designed this morning to set out for Bristol but was unexpectedly prevented. In the afternoon I received a letter from Leicestershire, pressing me to come without delay and pay the last office of friendship to one whose soul was on the wing for eternity. On Thursday, 20, I set out. The next afternoon I stopped a little at Newport-Pagnell and then rode on till I overtook a serious man, with whom I immediately fell into conversation.

Notice the urgency. Wesley did not embark on relationship evangelism. If we believe that a sinner could die at any moment and be swept into hell for eternity, we dare not let fear stop us from witnessing. Jesus didn't sit thus on the well for three months, building a relationship with the woman at the well in John Chapter 4. He spoke of water, then, He immediately swung to the subject of her eternal salvation.—Ray Comfort

He presently gave me to know what his opinions were: therefore I said nothing to contradict them. But that did not content him: he was quite uneasy to know whether I held the doctrine of the decrees as he did; but I told him over and over, "We had better keep to practical things, lest we should be angry at one another." And so we did for two miles, till he caught me unawares, and dragged me into the dispute before I knew where I was. He then grew warmer and warmer; told me I was rotten at heart suppose I was one of John Wesley's followers. I told him, "No, I am John Wesley himself." Upon which he would gladly have run away outright. But being better mounted of the two, I kept close to his side and endeavored to show him his heart, till we came into the street of Northampton.

Doesn't this warm your heart. Wesley wouldn't let this man get away. Be like that. It is said that the bulldog has its teeth slanted so that it can hold onto something and still keep breathing. We dare not let go of sinners if they have a slight ear to listen.—Ray Comfort

When Sin Abounds

THURSDAY, 27 – We came to Newcastle about six; and, after a short refreshment, walked into the town. I was surprised: so much drunkenness, cursing, and swearing (even from the mouths of little children) do I never remember to have seen and heard before, in so small a compass of time. Surely this place is ripe for Him who "came not to call the righteous, but sinners to repentance."

This is the heart of a true Christian. Most of the Church stay away from the darkness. That's where Wesley took the light.—Ray Comfort

SUNDAY, 30 – At seven I walked down to Sandgate, the poorest and most contemptible part of the town and, standing at the end of the street with John Taylor, began to sing the Hundredth Psalm. Three or four people came out to see what was the matter, the number soon increasing to four or five hundred.

If I could sing, I would sing to attract the lost. Use whatever God-given talents you have to get the ear of the lost. —Ray Comfort

I suppose there might be twelve or fifteen hundred before I had done preaching, to whom I applied those solemn words, "He was wounded for our transgressions, he was bruised for our iniquities: the chastisement of our peace was upon him; and with his stripes we are healed" [Isaiah 53:5].

The Righteousness of the Law

SATURDAY, 12 – I preached on the righteousness of the law and the righteousness of faith. While I was speaking, several dropped down as dead, and among the rest such a cry was heard of sinners groaning for the righteousness of faith as almost drowned my voice. But many of these soon lifted up their heads with joy and broke into thanksgiving, being assured they new had the desire of their soul—the forgiveness of their sins.

Would to God that would happen today when the Word is preached in truth.—Ray Comfort

⁂

Fruit Takes Time

At six I preached for the last time in Epworth churchyard (planning to leave the town the next morning) to a vast multitude gathered together from all parts, on the beginning of our Lord's Sermon on the Mount. I continued among them for nearly three hours, and yet we scarcely knew how to part. Oh, let none think his labor of love is lost because the fruit does not immediately appear! Nearly forty years did my father labor here, but he saw little fruit of all his labor. I took some pains among this people too, and my strength also seemed spent in vain; but now the fruit appeared. There were scarcely any in the town on whom either my father or I had taken any pains formerly but the seed, sown so long since, now sprang up, bringing forth repentance and remission of sins.

⁂

The Borders of Eternity

I left Bristol in the evening of Sunday, July 18, and on Tuesday came to London. I found my mother on the borders of eternity. But she had no doubt or fear nor any desire but (as soon as God should call) "to depart and be with Christ."

Friday, 23 – About three in the afternoon I went to my mother and found her change was near. I sat down on the bedside. She was in her last conflict, unable to speak but I believe quite sensible. Her look was calm and serene, and her eyes fixed upward while we commended her soul to God. From three to four the silver cord was loosing, and the wheel breaking at the cistern; and then without any struggle, or sigh, or groan, the soul was set at liberty. We stood round the bed and fulfilled her last request, uttered a little before she lost her speech: "Children, as soon as I am released, sing a psalm of praise to God."

Words cannot express the consolation that the Christian has in the face of death. It is no longer a darkened door to damnation, but a door that opens to everlasting pleasure.
—*Ray Comfort*

His Mother's Death

I cannot yet dismiss this subject. As self-will is the root of all sin and misery, so whatever cherishes this in children insures their after-wretchedness and irreligion; whatever checks and mortifies it promotes their future happiness and piety. This is still more evident if we further consider that religion is nothing else than the doing the will of God and not our own: that the one grand impediment to our temporal and eternal happiness being this self-will, no indulgences of it can be trivial, no denial unprofitable; and does all that in him lies to damn his child, soul and body forever.

Lost Shoe, Found an Ear

MONDAY, AUGUST 22 (LONDON) – After a few of us had joined in prayer, about four I set out, and rode softly to Snow Hill; where the saddle slipping quite upon my mare's neck, I fell over her head, and she ran back into Smithfield. Some boys caught her and brought her to me again, cursing and swearing all the way. I spoke plainly to them, and they promised to amend. I was setting forward when a man cried, "Sir you have lost your saddle-cloth." Two or three more would needs help me to put it on; but these too swore at almost every word. I turned to one and another and spoke in love. They all took it well and thanked me much. I gave them two or three little books, which they promised to read over carefully.

Before I reached Kensington, I found my mare had lost a shoe. This gave me an opportunity of talking closely, for nearly half an hour, both to the smith and his servant. I mention these little circumstances to show how easy it is to redeem every fragment of time (if I may so speak), when we feel any love to those souls for which Christ died.

The Way of Holiness

TUESDAY, 20 – At Trezuthan Downs I preached to two or three thousand people on the "highway" of the Lord, the way of holiness. We reached Gwennap a little before six and found the plain covered from end to end. It was supposed there were ten thousand people, to whom I preached Christ our "wisdom, righteousness, sanctification, and redemption." I could not conclude till it was so dark we could scarcely see one another. And there was on all sides the deepest attention; none speaking, stirring, or scarcely looking aside. Surely here, though in a temple not made with hands, was God worshiped in "the beauty of holiness."

WEDNESDAY, 21 – I was awakened between three and four by a large company of sinners who, fearing they should be too late, had gathered round the house and were singing and praising God. At five I preached once more on "Believe on the Lord Jesus Christ, and thou shalt be saved." They all devoured the Word. Oh, may it be health to their soul and marrow unto their bones!

Another Mob

THURSDAY, OCTOBER. 20 – After preaching to a small, attentive congregation (at Birmingham), I rode to Wednesbury. At twelve I preached in a ground near the middle of the town, to a far larger congregation than was expected, on "Jesus Christ, the same yesterday, and today, and forever" [Hebrews. 13:8]. I believe everyone present felt the power of God: and no creature offered to molest us, either going or coming; but the Lord fought for us, and we held our peace.

I was writing at Francis Ward's, in the afternoon, when the cry arose that the mob had beset the house. We prayed that God would disperse them; and it was so: one went this way, and another that; so that, in half an hour, not a man was left. I told our brethren, "Now is the time for us to go"; but they pressed me exceedingly to stay. So, that I might not offend them, I sat down; though I foresaw what would follow. Before five the mob surrounded the house again in greater numbers than ever. The cry of one and all was "Bring out the minister; we will have the minister."

I desired one to take their captain by the hand and bring him into the house. After a few sentences interchanged between us, the lion became a lamb. I desired him to go and bring one or two more of the most angry of his companions. He brought in two who were ready to swallow the ground with rage; but in two minutes they were as calm as he. I then bade them make way that I might go out among the people.

As soon as I was in the midst of them, I called for a chair; and standing up, asked, "What do any of you want with me?" Some said, "We want you to go with us to the justice." I replied, "That I will, with all my heart." I then spoke a few words, which God applied; so that they cried out, with might and main, "The gentleman is an honest gentleman, and we will spill our blood in his defense." I asked, "Shall we go to the justice tonight, or in the morning?" Most of them cried, "Tonight, tonight"; on which I went before, and two or three hundred followed; the rest returning whence they came.

The night came on before we had walked a mile, together with heavy rain. However, on we went to Bentley Hall, two miles from Wednesbury. One or two ran before to tell Mr. Lane they had brought Mr. Wesley before his worship. Mr. Lane replied, "What have I to do with Mr. Wesley? Go and carry him back again." By this time the main body came up and began knocking at the door. A servant told them Mr. Lane was in bed. His son followed and asked what was the matter. One replied, "Why, an't please you, they sing psalms all day; nay, and make folks rise at five in the morning. And what would your worship advise us to do?" "To go home," said Mr. Lane, "and be quiet."

✥

Wesley in Danger

H ere they were all at a full stop, till one advised to go to Justice Persehouse at Walsal. All agreed to this; so we hastened on and about seven came to his house. But Mr. P——likewise sent word that he was in bed. Now they were at a stand again; but at last they all thought it the wisest course to make the best of their way home. About fifty of them undertook to convoy me. But we had not gone a hundred yards when the mob of Walsal came, pouring in like a flood, and bore down all before them. The Darlaston mob made what defense they could; but they were weary as well as outnumbered, so that in a short time, many being knocked down, the rest ran away and left me in their hands.

To attempt speaking was vain, for the noise on every side was like the roaring of the sea. So they dragged me along till we came to the town; where seeing the door of a large house open, I attempted to go in; but a man, catching me by the hair, pulled me back into the middle of the mob. They made no more stops till they had carried me through the main street, from one end of the town to the other. I continued speaking all the time to those within hearing, feeling no pain or weariness. At the west end of the town, seeing a door half open, I made toward it and would have gone in; but a gentleman in the shop would not suffer me, saying they would pull the house down to the ground. However, I stood at the door, and asked,

"Are you willing to hear me speak?" Many cried out, "No, no! Knock his brains out; down with him; kill him at once." Others said, "Nay, but we will hear him first." I began asking, "What evil have I done? Which of you all have I wronged in word or deed?" And continued speaking for above a quarter of an hour, till my voice suddenly failed: then the floods began to lift up their voice again; many crying out, "Bring him away! Bring him away!"

In the meantime my strength and my voice returned, and I broke out aloud in prayer. And now the man who just before headed the mob turned and said, "Sir, I will spend my life for you: follow me, and not one soul here shall touch a hair of your head." Two or three of his fellows confirmed his words and got close to me immediately. At the same time, the gentleman in the shop cried out, "For shame, for shame! Let him go."

An honest butcher, who was a little farther off, said it was a shame they should do thus; and he pulled back four or five, one after another, who were running on the most fiercely. The people then, as if it had been by common consent, fell back to the right and left, while those three or four men took me between them and carried me through them all. But on the bridge the mob rallied again: we therefore went on one side, over the milldam, and thence through the meadows; till, a little before ten, God brought me safe to Wednesbury; I having lost only one flap of my waistcoat and a little skin from one of my hands.

"I look on all the world as my parish; thus far I mean, that, in whatever part of it I am, I judge it meet, right, and my bounden duty, to declare unto all that are willing to hear, the glad tidings of salvation."

This is so biblical. Look on this dying world as you ministry. Don't wait for a "calling." We have been told to go into all the world and preach the gospel to every creature (Mark 16:15). Go. —Ray Comfort

Have We a Burning Zeal?

A re we taught of God, that we may be able to teach others also? Do we know God? Do we know Jesus Christ? Hath "God revealed his Son in us?" And hath he "made us able ministers of the new covenant?" Where then are the "seals of our apostleship?" Who, that were dead in trespasses and sins, have been quickened by our word? Have we a burning zeal to save souls from death, so that for their sake we often forget even to eat our bread? Do we speak plain, "by manifestation of the truth commending ourselves to every man's conscience in the sight of God" (2 Corinthians. 4:2)?"

John Wesley, *The Sermons of John Wesley*, 1872 Edition (Thomas Jackson, editor).

"I value all things only by the price they shall gain in eternity."

Humility

"Let there be in you that lowly mind which was in Christ Jesus and be ye likewise clothed with humility. As one instance of this, be always ready to own any fault you have been in. If you have at any time thought, spoken or acted wrong, be not backward to acknowledge it. Never dream that this will hurt the cause of God; no, it will further it. Be therefore open and frank when you are taxed with anything; do not seek either to evade or disguise it; but let it appear just as it is, and you will thereby not hinder but adorn the Gospel."

Conscience

First, it is a witness—testifying what we have done, in though, or word, or action. Secondly, it is a judge —passing sentence on what we have done, that it is good or evil. And, thirdly, it, in some sort, executes the sentence, by occasioning a degree of complacency in him that does well, and a degree of uneasiness in him that does evil.

A person is doing something which the Scripture clearly forbids. You ask, "How do you dare to do this?" And are answered with perfect unconcern, "O, my heart does not condemn me." I reply, "So much the worse. I would to God it did! You would then be in a safer state than you are now. It is a dreadful thing to be condemned by the word of God, and yet not to be condemned by your own heart!" If we can break the least of the known commands of God, without any self-condemnation, it is plain that the god of this world hath hardened our hearts. If we do not soon recover from this, we shall be "past feeling," and our consciences (as St. Paul speaks) will be "seared as with a hot iron."

Conscience is placed in the middle, under God, and above man. It is a kind of silent reasoning of the mind, whereby those things which are judged to be right are approved of with pleasure; but those which are judged evil are disapproved of with uneasiness. This is a tribunal in the breast of men, to accuse sinners, and excuse them that do well.

John Wesley The Sermons of John Wesley, 1872 Edition

⚜

More on the Conscience

B ut here let no man deceive his own soul. "It is diligently to be noted, the faith which brings not forth repentance, and love, and all good works, is not that right living faith, but a dead and devilish one. For, even the devils believe that Christ was born of a virgin: that he wrought all kinds of miracles, declaring himself very God: that, for our sakes, he suffered a most painful death, to redeem us from death everlasting; that he rose again the third day: that he ascended into heaven, and sits at the right hand of the Father and at the end of the world shall come again to judge both the quick and dead. These articles of our faith the devils believe, and so they believe all that is written in the Old and New Testament. And yet for all this faith, they are but devils. They remain still in their damnable estate lacking the very true Christian faith."

The Sermons of John Wesley, 1872 Edition

Prayer

A continual desire is a continual prayer—that is, in a low sense of the word; for there is a far higher sense, such an open intercourse with God, such a close, uninterrupted communion with Him ...."

John Wesley (*Kneeling we Triumph book one*)

"The neglect of prayer is a grand hindrance to holiness."

Fasting

"There is something remarkable in the manner wherein God revived His work in these parts. A few months ago the generality of people in this circuit were exceeding lifeless. Samuel Meggot, perceiving this, advised the society at Barnard Castle to observe every Friday with fasting and prayer. The very first Friday they met together and God broke in upon them in a wonderful manner; and neighboring societies heard of this, agreed to follow the same rule, and soon experienced the same blessing. Is not the neglect of this plain duty (I mean, fasting, ranked by our Lord with almsgiving and prayer) one general occasion of deadness among Christians? Can anyone willingly neglect it, and be guiltless?"

John Wesley (*Kneeling we Triumph book one*)

"Bear up the hands that hang down, by faith and prayer; support the tottering knees. Have you any days of fasting and prayer? Storm the throne of grace and persevere therein, and mercy will come down."

"If I cannot see Thy face and live, then let me see Thy face and die."

"Tell me, how it is that in this room there are three candles and but one light, and I will explain to you the mode of the Divine existence."

I have a thought. I am a creature of a day, passing through life as an arrow through the air. I am a spirit come from God, and returning to God; just hovering over the great gulf; till a few moments hence, I am no more seen! I drop into an unchangeable eternity!

"Christianity is essentially a social religion, and that to turn it into a solitary religion is indeed to destroy it."

"My ground is the Bible. Yea, I am a Bible-bigot. I follow it in all things, both great and small."

"Once in seven years I burn all my sermons; for it is a shame if I cannot write better sermons now than I did seven years ago."

"Do all the good you can,

by all the means you can,

in all the ways you can,

in all the places you can,

at all the times you can,

to all the people you can,

as long as you ever can."

In the beginning of the year 1738, as I was returning from thence, the cry of my heart was, O grant that nothing in my soul may dwell, but thy pure love alone! O may thy love possess me whole, My joy, my treasure, and my crown! Strange fires far from my heart remove; My every act, word, thought, be love!

The best of it is, God is with us. "

"I am not afraid that the people called Methodists should ever cease to exist either in Europe or America. But I am afraid lest they should only exist as a dead sect, having the form of religion without the power. And this undoubtedly will be the case unless they hold fast the doctrine, spirit, and discipline with which they first set out."

———

How sad that this is what has become of the Methodist church.—Ray Comfort

———

"I have learned that true Christianity consists, not in a set of options, or of forms and ceremonies, but in holiness of heart and life."

"I desired as many as could to join together in fasting and prayer, that God would restore the spirit of love and of a sound mind to the poor deluded rebels in America"

"Lord, make yourself always present to my mind, and let your love fill and rule my soul in all those places, companies and employments to which You call me. Amen"

"The sea is an excellent figure of the fullness of God, and that of the blessed Spirit. For as the rivers all return into the sea; so the bodies, the souls, and the good works of the righteous, return into God, to live there in his eternal repose."
"Although all the graces of God depend on his mere bounty, yet is He pleased generally to attach them to the prayers, the instructions, and the holiness of those with whom we are. By strong though invisible attractions He draws some souls through their intercourse with others."

"The sympathies formed by grace far surpass those formed by nature."

"The truly devout show that passions as naturally flow from true as from false love; so deeply sensible are they of the goods and evils of those whom they love for God's sake. But this can only be comprehended by those who understand the language of love."

"The bottom of the soul may be in repose, even while we are in many outward troubles; just as the bottom of the sea is calm, while the surface is strongly agitated."

"The best helps to growth in grace are the ill usage, the affronts, and the losses which befall us. We should receive them with all thankfulness, as preferable to all others, were it only on this account – that our will has no part therein."

"The readiest way to escape from our sufferings is, to be willing they should endure as long as God pleases."

"If we suffer persecution and affliction in a right manner, we attain a larger measure of conformity to Christ, by a due improvement of one of these occasions, than we could have done merely by imitating his mercy in abundance of good works."

"One of the greatest evidences of God's love to those that love him is to send them afflictions with grace to bear them."
"Even in the greatest afflictions, we ought to testify to God that, in receiving them from his hand, we feel pleasure in the midst of the pain, from being afflicted by Him who loves us, and whom we love."

———•◦•———

I found that when I went through a terrible and dark experience that lasted for about a year, I was still able to share my faith. Don't let discouragement settle on you. Keep reaching out to the lost not matter what you come up against in life. You are a firefighter, and a firefighter doesn't let his own trials stop him from climbing a ladder to rescue the perishing.—Ray Comfort

———•◦•———

"The readiest way which God takes to draw a man to himself is to afflict him in that he loves most, and with good reason; and to cause this affliction to arise from some good action done with a single eye; because nothing can more clearly show him the emptiness of what is most lovely and desirable in the world."

"True resignation consists in a thorough conformity to the whole will of God, who wills and does all (excepting sin) which comes to pass in the world. In order to this we have only to embrace all events, good and bad, as His will."

"In the greatest afflictions which can befall the just, either from heaven or earth, they remain immovable in peace, and perfectly submissive to God, by an inward, loving regard to Him, uniting in one all the powers of their souls."

"We ought quietly to suffer whatever befalls us, to bear the defects of others and our own, to confess them to God in secret prayer, or with groans which cannot be uttered; but never to speak a sharp or peevish word, nor to murmur or repine; but thoroughly willing that God should treat you in the manner that pleases him. We are his lambs, and therefore ought to be ready to suffer, even to the death, without complaining."

"We are to bear with those we cannot amend, and to be content with offering them to God. This is true resignation. And since He has borne our infirmities, we may well bear those of each other for His sake."

"To abandon all, to strip one's self of all, in order to seek and to follow Jesus Christ naked to Bethlehem, where he was born; naked to the hall where he was scourged; and naked to Calvary, where he died on the cross, is so great a mercy, that neither the thing, nor the knowledge of it is given to any, but through faith in the Son of God."

"There is no love of God without patience, and no patience without lowliness and sweetness of spirit."

"Humility and patience are the surest proofs of the increase of love."

"Humility alone unites patience with love, without which it is impossible to draw profit from suffering; or indeed, to avoid complaint, especially when we think we have given no occasion for what men make us suffer."

"True humility is a kind of self-annihilation, and this is the centre of all virtues."

"A soul returned to God ought to be attentive to everything which is said to him, on the head of salvation, with a desire to profit thereby."

"Of the sins which God has pardoned, let nothing remain but a deeper humility in the heart, and a stricter regulation in our words, in our actions, and in our sufferings."

"The bearing men, and suffering evils in meekness and silence, is the sum of a Christian life."

"God is the first object of our love: Its next office is, to bear the defects of others. And we should begin the practice of this amidst our own household."

"We should chiefly exercise our love towards them who most shock either our way of thinking, or our temper, or our knowledge, or the desire we have, that others should be as virtuous as we wish to be ourselves."

"God hardly gives his Spirit even to those whom he has established in grace, if they do not pray for it on all occasions, not only once, but many times."

"God does nothing but in answer to prayer; and even they who have been converted to God without praying for it themselves, (which is exceeding rare,) were not without the prayers of others. Every new victory which a soul gains is the effect of a new prayer."

"On every occasion of uneasiness, we should retire to prayer, that we may give place to the grace and light of God; and then form our resolutions, without being in any pain about what success they may have."

In the greatest temptations, a single look to Christ, and the barely pronouncing his name, suffices to overcome the wicked one, so it be done with confidence and calmness of spirit."

"God's command to 'pray without ceasing' is founded on the necessity we have of his grace to preserve the life of God in the soul, which can no more subsist one moment without it, than the body can without air."

Whether we think of or speak to God, whether we act or suffer for him, all is prayer, when we have no other object than his love, and the desire of pleasing him.

"All that a Christian does, even in eating and sleeping, is prayer, when it is done in simplicity, according to the order of God, without either adding to or diminishing from it by his own choice."

"Prayer continues in the desire of the heart, though the understanding be employed on outward things."

"In souls filled with love, the desire to please God is a continual prayer."

"As the furious hate which the devil bears us is termed the roaring of a lion, so our vehement love may be termed crying after God."

"God only requires of his adult children, that their hearts be truly purified, and that they offer him continually the wishes and vows that naturally spring from perfect love. For these desires, being the genuine fruits of love, are the most perfect prayers that can spring from it."

It is scarce conceivable how strait the way is wherein God leads them that follow him; and how dependent on him we must be, unless we are wanting in our faithfulness to him.

"It is hardly credible of how great consequence before God the smallest things are; and what great inconveniences sometimes follow those which appear to be light faults.

"As a very little dust will disorder a clock, and the least sand will obscure our sight, so the least grain of sin which is upon the heart will hinder its right motion towards God."

"We ought to be in the church as the saints are in heaven, and in the house as the holiest men are in the church; doing our work in the house as we pray in the church; worshipping God from the ground of the heart."

"We should be continually laboring to cut off all the useless things that surround us; and God usually retrenches the superfluities of our souls in the same proportion as we do those of our bodies."

"The best means of resisting the devil is to destroy whatever of the world remains in us, in order to raise for God, upon its ruins, a building all of love. Then shall we begin, in this fleeting life, to love God as we shall love him in eternity."

"We scarce conceive how easy it is to rob God of His due, in our friendship with the most virtuous persons, until they are torn from us by death. But if this loss produce lasting sorrow, that is a clear proof that we had before two treasures, between which we divided our heart."

"If, after having renounced all, we do not watch incessantly, and beseech God to accompany our vigilance with his, we shall be again entangled and overcome."

"As the most dangerous winds may enter at little openings, so the devil never enters more dangerously than by little unobserved incidents, which seem to be nothing, yet insensibly open the heart to great temptations."

"It is good to renew ourselves, from time to time, by closely examining the state of our souls, as if we had never done it before; for nothing tends more to the full assurance of faith, than to keep ourselves by this means in humility, and the exercise of all good works."

"To continual watchfulness and prayer ought to be added continual employment. For grace fills a vacuum as well as nature; and the devil fills whatever God does not fill."

"There is no faithfulness like that which ought to be between a guide of souls and the person directed by him. They ought continually to regard each other in God, and closely to examine themselves, whether all their thoughts are pure, and all their words directed with Christian discretion. Other affairs are only the things of men; but these are peculiarly the things of God."

"The words of St. Paul, 'No man can call Jesus Lord, but by the Holy Ghost,' show us the necessity of eyeing God in our good works, and even in our minutest thoughts; knowing that none are pleasing to him, but those which he forms in us and with us. From hence we learn that we cannot serve him, unless he use our tongue, hands, and heart, to do by himself and his Spirit whatever he would have us to do."

"If we were not utterly impotent, our good works would be our own property; whereas now they belong wholly to God, because they proceed from him and his grace: While raising our works, and making them all divine, he honors himself in us through them.

"One of the principal rules of religion is, to lose no occasion of serving God. And, since he is invisible to our eyes, we are to serve him in our neighbor; which he receives as if done to himself in person, standing visibly before us."

"God does not love men that are inconstant, nor good works that are intermitted. Nothing is pleasing to him, but what has a resemblance of his own immutability."

"A constant attention to the work which God entrusts us with is a mark of solid piety."

"Love fasts when it can, and as much as it can. It leads to all the ordinances of God, and employs itself in all the outward works whereof it is capable. It flies, as it were, like Elijah over the plain, to find God upon his holy mountain."

"God is so great, that he communicates greatness to the least thing that is done for his service."

"Happy are they who are sick, yea, or lose their life, for having done a good work."

"God frequently conceals the part which his children have in the conversion of other souls. Yet one may boldly say, that person who long groans before him for the conversion of another, whenever that soul is converted to God, is one of the chief causes of it."

Good Works

Charity cannot be practiced right, unless first we exercise it the moment God gives the occasion; and second, retire the instant after to offer it to God by humble thanksgiving. And this for three reasons: First, to render him what we have received from him. The Second, to avoid the dangerous temptation which springs from the very goodness of these works. And the Third, to unite ourselves to God, in whom the soul expands itself in prayer, with all the graces we have received, and the good works we have done, to draw from him new strength against the bad effects which these very works may produce in us, if we do not make use of the antidotes which God has ordained against these poisons. The true means to be filled anew with the riches of grace is thus to strip ourselves of it; and without this it is extremely difficult not to grow faint in the practice of good works.

"Good works do not receive their last perfection till they, as it were, lose themselves in God. This is a kind of death to them, resembling that of our bodies, which will not attain their highest life, their immortality, till they lose themselves in the glory of our souls, or rather of God, wherewith they shall be filled. And it is only what they had of earthly and mortal, which good works lose by this spiritual death."

Gratitude and Good Works

Fire is the symbol of love; and the love of God is the principle and the end of all our good works. But truth surpasses figure; and the fire of divine love has this advantage over material fire, that it can re-ascend to its source, and raise thither with it all the good works which it produces. And by this means it prevents their being corrupted by pride, vanity, or any evil mixture. But this cannot be done otherwise than by making these good works in a spiritual manner die in God, by a deep gratitude, which plunges the soul in him as in an abyss, with all that it is, and all the grace and works for which it is indebted to him; a gratitude whereby the soul seems to empty itself of them, that they may return to their source, as rivers seem willing to empty themselves, when they pour themselves with all their waters into the sea."

God the Source

When we have received any favor from God, we ought to retire, if not into our closets, into our hearts, and say, 'I come, Lord, to restore to you what you have given; and I freely relinquish it, to enter again into my own nothingness. For what is the most perfect creature in heaven or earth in thy presence, but a void capable of being filled with thee and by thee; as the air, which is void and dark, is capable of being filled with the light of the sun, who withdraws it every day to restore it the next, there being nothing in the air that either appropriates this light or resists it? O give me the same facility of receiving and restoring thy grace and good works! I say, **yours;** for I acknowledge the root from which they spring is in you, and not in me.'"

Another Angry Mob

THURSDAY, 4 – I rode to Falmouth. About three in the afternoon I went to see a gentlewoman who had been long indisposed. Almost as soon as I sat down, the house was beset on all sides by an innumerable multitude of people. A louder or more confused noise could hardly be at the taking of a city by storm. At first Mrs. B. and her daughter endeavored to quiet them. But it was labor lost. They might as well have attempted to still the raging of the sea. They were soon glad to shift for themselves and leave K. E. and me to do as well as we could. The rabble roared with all their throats, 'Bring out the Canorum! Where is the Canorum?' (An unmeaning word which the Cornish generally use instead of Methodist).

No answer being given, they quickly forced open the outer door and filled the passage. Only a wainscot partition was between us, which was not likely to stand long. I immediately took down a large looking glass which hung against it, supposing the whole side would fall in at once. When they began their work with abundance of bitter imprecations, poor Kitty was utterly astonished and cried out, "O sir, what must we do?" I said, "We must pray." Indeed at that time, to all appearance, our lives were not worth an hour's purchase. She asked, "But, sir, is it not better for you to hide yourself? To get into the closet?" I answered, "No. It is best for me to stand just where I am." Among those without were the crews of privateers which were lately come into harbor. Some of these, being angry at the slowness of the rest, thrust them away and, coming up all together, set their shoulders to the inner door and cried out, "Avast, lads, avast!" Away went all the hinges at once, and the door fell back into the room.

I stepped forward at once into the midst of them and said, "Here I am. Which of you has anything to say to me? To which of you have I done any wrong? To you? Or you? Or you?" I continued speaking till I came, bareheaded as I was (for I purposely left my hat that they might all see my face) into the middle of the street, and then raising my voice said, "Neighbors, countrymen! Do you desire to hear me speak?" They cried vehemently, "Yes, yes. He shall speak. He shall. Nobody shall hinder him." But having nothing to stand on and no advantage of ground, I could be heard by few only. However, I spoke without intermission and, as far as the sound reached, the people were still; till one or two of their captains turned about and swore that not a man should touch me.

Dirt Throwers

FRIDAY, 12 – After preaching at Oakhill, about noon I rode to Shepton and found them all under a strange consternation. A mob, they said, was hired, prepared, and made sufficiently drunk, in order to do all manner of mischief. I began preaching between four and five; none hindered or interrupted at all. We had blessed opportunity, and the hearts of many were exceedingly comforted. I wondered what was become of the mob. But we were quickly informed: they mistook the place, imagining I should alight (as I used to do) at William Stone's house, and had summoned, by drum, all their forces together to meet me at my coming; but Mr. Swindells innocently carrying me to the other end of the town, they did not find their mistake till I had done preaching; so that the hindering this, which was one of their designs, was utterly disappointed.

However, they attended us from the preaching house to William Stone's, throwing dirt, stones, and clods in abundance; but they could not hurt us. Only Mr. Swindells had a little dirt on his coat, and I a few specks on my hat.

After we were gone into the house, they began throwing great stones, in order to break the door. But perceiving this would require some time, they dropped that design for the present. They first broke all the tiles on the penthouse over the door and then poured in a shower of stones at the windows. One of their captains, in his great zeal, had followed us into the house and was now shut in with us. He did not like this and would fain have got out; but it was not possible; so he kept as close to me as he could, thinking himself safe when he was near me; but, staying a little behind—when I went up two pair of stairs and stood close on one side where we were a little sheltered—a stone struck him on the forehead, and the blood spouted out like a stream. He cried out, "O sir, are we to die tonight? What must I do? What must I do?" I said, "Pray to God. He is able to deliver you from all danger." He took my advice and began praying in such a manner as he had scarcely done ever since he was born.

Modern preachers need never fear this happening. They tickle the ears of the world with the words, and the world loves it. Wesley didn't compromise and he had the same hatred leveled at him as his Master had at Him.—Ray Comfort

Mr. Swindells and I then went to prayer; after which I told him, "We must not stay here; we must go down immediately." He said, "Sir, we cannot stir; you see how the stones fly about." I walked straight through the room and down the stairs; and not a stone came in, till we were at the bottom. The mob had just broken open the door when we came into the lower room; and exactly while they burst in at one door, we walked out at the other. Nor did one man take any notice of us, though we were within five yards of each other.

The Highest Indecency

I wonder at those who still talk so loud of the indecency of field-preaching. The highest indecency is in St. Paul's Church, when a considerable part of the congregation are asleep, or talking, or looking about, not minding a word the preacher says. On the other hand, there is the highest decency in a churchyard or field, when the whole congregation behave and look as if there was the Judge of all and heard Him speaking from heaven.

Utterly Wild

At one I went to the Cross in Bolton. There was a vast number of people, but many of them utterly wild. As soon as I began speaking, they began thrusting to and fro, endeavoring to throw me down from the steps on which I stood. They did so once or twice; but I went up again and continued my discourse. They then began to throw stones; at the same time some got up on the Cross behind me to push me down; on which I could not but observe how God overrules even the minutest circumstances. One man was bawling just at my ear, when a stone struck him on the cheek and he was still. A second was forcing his way down to me till another stone hit him on the forehead; it bounded back, the blood ran down, and he came no farther. The third, being close to me, stretched out his hand, and in the instant a sharp stone came upon the joints of his fingers. He shook his hand and was very quiet till I concluded my discourse and went away.

A Mob Bursts into the House

We came to Bolton about five in the evening. We had no sooner entered the main street than we perceived the lions at Rochdale were lambs in comparison to those at Bolton. Such rage and bitterness I scarcely ever saw before in any creatures that bore the form of men. They followed us in full cry to the house where we went; and as soon as we had gone in, took possession of all the avenues to it and filled the street from one end to the other.

After some time the waves did not roar quite so loud. Mr. P—— thought he might then venture out. They immediately closed in, threw him down and rolled him in the mire; so that when he scrambled from them and got into the house again, one could scarcely tell what or who he was. When the first stone came among us through the window, I expected a shower to follow; and the rather, because they had now procured a bell to call their whole forces together. But they did not design to carry on the attack at a distance; presently one ran up and told us the mob had burst into the house; he added that they had got J——B——in the midst of them. They had; and he laid hold on the opportunity to tell them of "the terrors of the Lord."

Meantime D——T—— engaged another part of them with smoother and softer words. Believing the time was now come, I walked down into the thickest of them. They had now filled all the rooms below. I called for a chair. The winds were hushed, and all was calm and still. My heart was filled with love, my eyes with tears, and my mouth with arguments.

They were amazed; they were ashamed; they were melted down; they devoured every word. What a turn was this! Oh, how did God change the counsel of the old Ahithophel into foolishness and bring all the drunkards, swearers, Sabbath-breakers, and mere sinners in the place, to hear of His plenteous redemption!

Different Talents

1750. SUNDAY, JANUARY 28 – I read prayers (in London), and Mr. Whitefield preached. How wise is God in giving different talents to different preachers! Even the little improprieties both of his language and manner were a means of profiting many, who would not have been touched by a more correct discourse, or a more calm and regular manner of speaking.

Distant Rabble

SUNDAY, MAY 20 (CORK) –Understanding the usual place of preaching would by no means contain those who desired to hear, about eight I went to Hammond's Marsh. The congregation was large and deeply attentive. A few of the rabble gathered at a distance; but by little and little they drew near and mixed with the congregation; I have seldom seen a more quiet and orderly assembly at any church in England or Ireland.

In the afternoon, a report being spread abroad that the mayor designed to hinder my preaching on the Marsh in the evening, I desired Mr. Skelton and Mr. Jones to wait upon him and inquire concerning it. Mr. Skelton asked if my preaching there would be disagreeable to him, adding, "Sir, if it would, Mr. Wesley will not do it." He replied warmly, "Sir, I'll have no mobbing." Mr. Skelton replied, "Sir, there was none this morning." He answered, "There was. Are there not churches and meetinghouses enough? I will have no more mobs or riots." Mr. Skelton replied, "Sir, neither Mr. Wesley nor they that heard him made either mobs or riots." He answered plainly, "I will have no more preaching; and if Mr. Wesley attempts to preach, I am prepared for him."

I began preaching in our own house soon after five. Mr. Mayor meantime was walking in the 'Change, and giving orders to the town drummers and to his sergeants—doubtless to go down and deep the peach! They accordingly came down to the house, with an innumerable mob attending them. They continued drumming, and I continued preaching till I had finished my discourse. When I came out, the mob immediately closed me in. Observing one of the sergeants standing by, I desired him to keep the King's peace; but he replied, "Sir, I have no orders to do that." As soon as I came into the street, the rabble threw whatever came to hand; but all went by me or flew over my head; nor do I remember that one thing touched me. I walked on straight through the midst of the rabble, looking every man before me in the face; and they opened on the right and left, till I came near Dant's Bridge. A large party had taken possession of this, one of whom was bawling out, "Now, hey for the Romans!" When I came up, they likewise shrank back, and I walked through them to Mr. Jenkins's house; but a Papist stood just within the door and endeavored to hinder my going in till one of the mob (I suppose aiming at me, but missing) knocked her down flat.

I then went in, and God restrained the wild beasts so that not one attempted to follow me.

But many of the congregation were more roughly handled, particularly Mr. Jones, who was covered with dirt and escaped with his life almost by miracle. The main body of the mob then went to the house, brought out all the seats and benches, tore up the floor, the door, the frames of the windows, and whatever of woodwork remained; part of which they carried off for their own use, and the rest they burned in the open street.

I have seen angry sinners smash my property. I have watched, thinking that I would have them take their wrath out on my property, rather than on me.—Ray Comfort

A Violent Storm

1752. SUNDAY, MARCH 15 (LONDON) – While I was preaching at West Street in the afternoon, there was one of the most violent storms I ever remember. In the midst of the sermon a great part of a house opposite to the chapel was blown down. We heard a huge noise but knew not the cause; so much the more did God speak to our hearts, and great was the rejoicing of many in confidence of His protection. Between four and five I took horse, with my wife and daughter. The tiles were rattling from the houses on both sides, but they hurt not us. We reached Hayes about seven in the evening, and Oxford the next day.

What Shall it Profit a Man

I went to prayers at three in the old church—a grand and venerable structure. Between five and six the coach called and took me to Mighton Car, about half a mile from the town. A huge multitude, rich and poor, horse and foot, with several coaches, were soon gathered together; to whom I cried with a loud voice and a composed spirit, "What shall it profit a man, if he shall gain the whole world, and lose his own soul?" Some thousands of the people seriously attended; but many behaved as if possessed by Moloch. Clods and stones flew about on every side; but they neither touched nor disturbed me.

When I had finished my discourse, I went to take coach, but the coachman had driven clear away. We were at a loss, till a gentlewoman invited my wife and me to come into her coach. She brought some inconveniences on herself thereby; not only as there were nine of us in the coach, three on each side, and three in the middle; but also as the mob closely attended us, throwing in at the windows (which we did not think it prudent to shut) whatever came next to hand. But a large gentlewoman who sat in my lap screened me, so that nothing came near me.

A Deep Hollow

TUESDAY, AUGUST 25 – I preached in the market place at Kinsale. The next morning at eight I walked to the fort. On the hill above it we found a large, deep hollow, capable of containing two or three thousand people. On one side of this, the soldiers soon cut a place with their swords for me to stand, where I was screened both from the wind and sun, while the congregation sat on the grass before me. Many eminent sinners were present, particularly of the army; and I believe God gave them a loud call to repentance.

If you begin open air preaching, you will look for places that are ideal for holding sound.—Ray Comfort

The Enemy's Defeat

MONDAY, SEPTEMBER 9 – I preached at Charlton, a village six miles from Taunton, to a large congregation gathered from the towns and country for many miles round. All the farmers here had some time before entered into a joint engagement to turn all out of their service and give no work to any who went to hear a Methodist preacher. But there is no counsel against the Lord. One of the chief of them, Mr. G——, was not long after convinced of the truth and desired those very men to preach at his house. Many of the other confederates came to hear, whom their servants and laborers gladly followed. So

the whole device of Satan fell to the ground; and the Word
of God grew and prevailed.

Hard Heart Softened

Thursday, 3 – I rode to Reading and preached in the evening.
Observing a warm man near the door (he was once of the
society), I purposely bowed to him; but he made no return.
During the first prayer he stood, but sat while we sang. In
the sermon his countenance changed, and in a little while
he turned his face to the wall. He stood at the second hymn
and then kneeled down. As I came out he caught me by the
hand and dismissed me with a hearty blessing.

Hand in Hand

WEDNESDAY, NOVEMBER 5 – Mr. Whitefield called upon me.
Disputings are now no more; we love one another and join
hand in hand to promote the cause of our common Master.

It Will Be Well With You

WEDNESDAY, 28 – I rode to Tullamore, where one of the society, Edward Willis, gave me a very surprising account of himself. He said:

"When I was about twenty years old, I went to Waterford for business. After a few weeks I resolved to leave it and packed up my things, in order to set out the next morning. This was Sunday, but my landlord pressed me much not to go till the next day. In the afternoon we walked out together and went into the river. After a while, leaving him near the shore, I struck out into the deep. I soon heard a cry and, turning, saw him rising and sinking in the channel of the river. I swam back with all speed and, seeing him sink again, dived down after him. When I was near the bottom, he clasped his arm around my neck and held me so fast that I could not rise.

"Seeing death before me, all my sins came into my mind and I faintly called for mercy. In a while my senses went away and I thought I was in a place full of light and glory, with abundance of people. While I was thus, who held me died, and I floated up to the top of the water. I then immediately came to myself and swam to the shore, where several stood who had seen us sink and said they never knew such a deliverance before; for I had been under water full twenty minutes. It made me more serious for two or three months. Then I returned to all my sins.

"But in the midst of all, I had a voice following me everywhere, 'When an able minister of the gospel comes, it will be well with you!' Some years after I entered into the army; our troop lay at Phillipstown, when Mr. W. came. I was much affected by his preaching, but not so as to leave my sins. The voice followed me still, and when Mr. J. W. came, before I saw him I had an unspeakable conviction that he was the man I looked for. Soon after I found peace with God, and it was well with me indeed."

Perhaps God has sinners waiting for you and me to speak to them.—Ray Comfort

---

Under the Gallows

TUESDAY, 11 – I was at a loss where to preach, the person who owned the loft refusing to let me preach there, or even in the yard below. And the commanding officer being asked for the use of the barrack-yard, answered, it was not a proper place. "Not," said he, "that I have any objection to Mr. Wesley. I will hear him if he preaches under the gallows." It remained to preach in the street, and by this means the congregation was more than doubled. Both the officers and soldiers gave great attention, till a poor man, special drunk, came marching down the street, attended by a popish mob, with a club in one hand and large cleaver in the other, grievously cursing and blaspheming, and swearing he would cut off the preacher's head. It was with difficulty that I restrained the troopers, especially them that were not of the society.

This is terribly frustrating. I remember the frustration of being among a crowd in Washington Square in New York. I simply wanted an old wooden box to stand on, and the owners refused. No one would lend or sell me a thing. When that happened it seemed that the whole world was against me. I still preached, without elevation, but it was difficult because it leaves you vulnerable.—Ray Comfort

When he came nearer, the mayor stepped out of the congregation and strove, by good words, to make him quiet; but he could not prevail. He went into his house and returned with his white wand. At the same time he sent for two constables, who presently came with their staves. He charged them not to strike the man unless he struck first; but this he did immediately, as soon as they came within his reach, and wounded one of them in the wrist. On this, the other knocked him down, which he did three times before he would submit. The mayor then walked before, the constables on either hand, and conducted him to the jail.

A Wanderer upon Earth

Monday, June 4 – After preaching (at Alnwick), I rode on to Newcastle. Certainly if I did not believe there was another world, I should spend all my summers here; I know no place in Great Britain comparable to it for pleasantness. But I seek another country and therefore am content to be a wanderer upon the earth.

Be in Earnest

THURSDAY, 21 – I preached at Nafferton at one. As I was riding thence, one stopped me on the road and said, "Sir, do you not remember, when you were at Prudhoe two years since and you breakfasted at Thomas Newton's? I am his sister. You looked upon me as you were going out, and said, 'Be in earnest.' I knew not then what earnestness meant, nor had any thought about it; but the words sank into my heart so that I could never rest any more till I sought and found Christ."

―――――•―•―•―――――

Never underestimate the power of the words you say for the gospel. I rarely let a wrong number go without saying, "Make sure you read your Bible." Sometimes that's all I get to say, other times I have been able to share a compete gospel message. We are planting seeds for eternity. A small seed of a word will grow into a mighty tree of righteousness, if God so sees fit.—Ray Comfort

The Devil and Fileld Preaching

On Monday and Tuesday evening I preached abroad, near the Keelman's Hospital, to twice the people we should have had at the house. What marvel the devil does not love field preaching? Neither do I: I love a commodious room, a soft cushion, a handsome pulpit. But where is my zeal if I do not trample all these underfoot in order to save one more soul?

I have to agree. I would rather step into a pulpit with thousands before me, good sound system and grateful applause, than stand on a box and speak to sinners who don't want to hear what I have to say. But I have no choice, if I want to reach the lost. With the help of God, I can reach more sinners on a good day of open air preaching than I can in ten services in a huge church building. —Ray Comfort

Are You Deaf?

WEDNESDAY, JULY 4 (HARTLEPOOL) – Mr. Jones preached at five, I at eight. Toward the close of the sermon, a queer, dirty, clumsy man, I suppose a country wit, took a deal of pains to disturb the congregation. When I had done, fearing he might hurt those who were gathered about him, I desired two or three of our brethren to go to him, one after the other, and not say much themselves but let him talk till he was weary. They did so, but without effect, as his fund of ribaldry seemed inexhaustible. W. A. then tried another way. He got into the circle close to him and listening a while said, "This is pretty; pray say it over again." "What! Are you deaf?" "No; but for the entertainment of the people. Come; we are all attention." After repeating this twice or thrice, the wag could not stand it; but, with two or three curses, walked clear off.

It's a little hard to figure what Wesley is saying, but it seemed to get rid of his annoyance. I have found an effective way to stop a crowd disruptor is to quietly ask him if he would like a free hamburger. They often do. I then have a brother take him for one, some distance away.—Ray Comfort

---

They will be Damned

About five in the afternoon I heard them singing hymns. Soon after, Mr. B. came up and told me Alice Miller (fifteen years old) had fallen into a trance. I went down immediately and found her sitting on a stool and leaning against the wall, with her eyes open and fixed upward. I made a motion as if going to strike, but they continued immovable. Her face showed an unspeakable mixture of reverence and love, while silent tears stole down her cheeks. Her lips were a little open, and sometimes moved; but not enough to cause any sound.

I do not know whether I ever saw a human face look so beautiful; sometimes it was covered with a smile, as from joy, mixing with love and reverence; but the tears fell still though not so fast. Her pulse was quite regular. In about half an hour I observed her countenance change into the form of fear, pity, and distress; then she burst into a flood of tears and cried out, "Dear Lord; they will be damned! They will all be damned!" But in about five minutes her smiles returned, and only love and joy appeared in her face.

About half an hour after six, I observed distress take place again; and soon after she wept bitterly and cried out, "Dear

Lord, they will go to hell! The world will go to hell!" Soon after, she said, "Cry aloud! Spare not!" And in a few moments her look was composed again and spoke a mixture of reverence, joy, and love. Then she said aloud, "Give God the glory." About seven her senses returned. I asked, "Where have you been?"—"I have been with my Savior." "In heaven, or on earth?"—"I cannot tell; but I was in glory." "Why then did you cry?"—"Not for myself, but for the world; for I saw they were on the brink of hell." "Whom did you desire to give the glory to God?"—"Ministers that cry aloud to the world; else they will be proud; and then God will leave them, and they will lose their own souls."

Lift Up Your Voice

SUNDAY, 23 – A vast majority of the immense congregation in Moorfields were deeply serious. One such hour might convince any impartial man of the expediency of field preaching. What building, except St. Paul's Church, would contain such a congregation? And if it would, what human voice could have reached them there? By repeated observations I find I can command thrice the number in the open air that I can under a roof. And who can say the time for field-preaching is over while 1) greater numbers that ever attend; 2) the converting, as well as convincing, power of God is eminently present with them?

I Have a Message

1760. WEDNESDAY, JANUARY 16 – One came to me, as she said, with a message from the Lord, to tell me that I was laying up treasures on earth, taking my ease, and minding only my eating and drinking. I told her God knew me better; and if He had sent her, He would have sent her with a more proper message.

Be ready for people that hear from God on your behalf. If things are right between you and God, He will speak to you Himself.—Ray Comfort

I Have Preached Already

TUESDAY, JUNE 10 – I rode to Drumersnave, a village delightfully situated. At noon William Ley, James Glasbrook, and I rode to Carrick-upon-Shannon. In less than an hour, an esquire and justice of the peace came down with a drum and what mob he could gather. I went into the garden with the congregation, while he was making a speech to his followers in the street. He then attacked William Ley (who stood at the door), being armed with a halberd and long sword, and ran at him with the halberd; but missing his thrust, he then struck at him and broke it short upon his wrist. Having made his way through the house to the other door, he was at a full stop. James Glasbrook held it fast on the other side.

While he was endeavoring to force it open, one told him I was preaching in the garden. On this he quitted the door in haste, ran round the house, and with part of his retinue, climbed over the wall into the garden; with a whole volley of oaths and curses declared, "You shall not preach here today." I told him, "Sir, I do not intend it, for I have preached already." This made him ready to tear the ground. Finding he was not to be reasoned with, I went into the house. Soon after he revenged himself on James Glasbrook (by breaking the truncheon of his halberd on his arm), and on my hat, which he beat and kicked most valiantly; but a gentleman rescued it out of his hands, and we rode quietly out of the town.

This is the same abundant life that the Apostle Paul experienced. —Ray Comfort

A Few Stones

SUNDAY, 5 – Believing one hindrance of the work of God in York was the neglect of field-preaching, I preached this morning at eight, in an open place near the city walls. Abundance of people ran together, most of whom were deeply attentive. One or two only were angry and threw a few stones; but it was labor lost; for none regarded them.

SUNDAY, 12 – I had appointed to be at Haworth; but the church would not nearly contain the people who came from all sides. However, Mr. Grimshaw had provided for this by fixing a scaffold on the outside of one of the windows, through which I went after prayers, and the people likewise all went out into the churchyard. The afternoon congregation was larger still. What has God wrought in the midst of those rough mountains!

Calm and Sober-minded

MONDAY, 26 – In some respects the work of God in Dublin was more remarkable than even that in London. 1) Greater, in proportion to the time and to the number of people. That society had above seven-and-twenty hundred members; this not a fifth part of the number. Six months after the flame broke out there, we had about thirty witnesses of the great salvation. In Dublin there were about forty in less than four months. 2) The work was more pure. In all this time, while they were mildly and tenderly treated, there were none of them headstrong or unadvisable; none that were wiser than their teachers; none who dreamed of being immortal or infallible or incapable of temptation: in short, no whimsical or enthusiastic persons; all were calm and sober-minded.

Not Fully Come

M any years ago my brother frequently said, "Your day of Pentecost is not fully come; but I doubt not it will; and you will then hear of persons sanctified as frequently as you do now of persons justified." Any unprejudiced reader may observe that it was now fully come. And accordingly we did hear of persons sanctified, in London and most other parts of England, and in Dublin and many other parts of Ireland, as frequently as of persons justified; although instances of the latter were far more frequent than they had been for twenty years before. That many of these did not retain the gift of God is no proof that it was not given them. That many do retain it to this day is matter of praise and thanksgiving. And many of them are gone to Him whom they loved, praising Him with their latest breath; just in the spirit on Ann Steed, the first witness in Bristol of the great salvation; who, being worn out with sickness and racking pain, after she had commended to God all that were round her, lifted up her eyes, cried aloud, "Glory! Hallelujah!" and died.

Worn Out Whitefield

1763. MONDAY, MAY 16 – Setting out a month later than usual, I judge it needful to make the more haste; so I took post chaises and by that means easily reached Newcastle on Wednesday, 18. Thence I went on at leisure and came to Edinburgh on Saturday, 21. The next day I had the satisfaction of spending a little time with Mr. Whitefield. Humanly speaking, he is worn out; but we have to do with Him who hath all power in heaven and earth.

See Whitefield Gold—Ray Comfort (Bridge Logos Publishers).

MONDAY, 23 – I rode to Forfar and on Tuesday, 24, rode on to Aberdeen.

A Change of Climate

WEDNESDAY, 25 – I inquired into the state of things here. Surely never was there a more open door. The four ministers of Aberdeen, the minister of the adjoining town, and the three ministers of Old Aberdeen, hitherto seem to have no dislike but rather to wish us "good luck in the name of the Lord." More of the townspeople as yet seem to wish us well, so that there is no open opposition of any kind. Oh, what spirit ought a preacher to be of that he may be able to bear all this sunshine!

About noon I went to Gordon's Hospital, built near the town for poor children. It is exceedingly clean. The gardens are pleasant, well laid out, and in extremely good order; but the old bachelor who founded it has expressly provided that no woman should ever be there.

At seven, the evening being fair and mild, I preached to a multitude of people in the College Close on "Stand ye in the ways, and see, and ask for the old paths" [Jeremiah. 6:16]. But the next evening, the weather being raw and cold, I preached in the College Hall. What an amazing willingness to hear runs through this whole kingdom! There want only a few zealous, active laborers, who desire nothing but God, and they might soon carry the gospel through all this country, even as high as the Orkneys.

❧❀❦

Plain Speaking

SUNDAY, 29 – I preached at seven in the High School yard, Edinburgh. It being the time of the General Assembly, which drew together not the ministers only, but abundance of the nobility and gentry, many of both sorts were present; but abundantly more at five in the afternoon. I spoke as plainly as ever I did in my life. But I never knew any in Scotland offended at plain dealing. In this respect the North Britons are a pattern to all mankind.

❧❀❦

Increasing Work

TUESDAY, JUNE 7 – There is something remarkable in the manner wherein God revived His work in these parts. A few months ago the generality of people in this circuit were exceedingly lifeless. Samuel Meggot, perceiving this, advised the society at Barnard Castle to observe every Friday with fasting and prayer. The very first Friday they met together, God broke in upon them in a wonderful manner; and His work has been increasing among them ever since. The neighboring societies heard of this, agreed to follow the same rule, and soon experienced the same blessing. Is not the neglect of this plain duty (I mean fasting, ranked by our Lord with almsgiving and prayer) one general occasion of deadness among Christians? Can anyone willingly neglect it and be guiltless?

Cursing the Preacher

THURSDAY, 16 – At five in the evening I preached at Dewsbury and on Friday, 17, reached Manchester. Here I received a particular account of a remarkable incident: An eminent drunkard of Congleton used to divert himself, whenever there was preaching there, by standing over against the house, cursing and swearing at the preacher. One evening he had a fancy to step in and hear what the man had to say. He did so, but it made him so uneasy that he could not sleep all night. In the morning he was more uneasy still; he walked in the fields, but all in vain, till it came in his mind to go to one of his merry companions, who was always ready to abuse the Methodists. He told him how he was and asked what he should do. "Do!" said Samuel, "go and join the society. I will; for I was never so uneasy in my life." They did so without delay. But presently David cried out, "I am sorry I joined; for I shall get drunk again, and they will turn me out." However, he stood firm for four days; on the fifth, he was persuaded by the old companions to "take one pint," and then another, and another, till one of them said, "See, here is a Methodist drunk!"

David started up, and knocked him over, chair and all. He then drove the rest out of the house, caught up the landlady, carried her out, threw her into the kennel; went back to the house, broke down the door, threw it into the street, and then ran into the fields, tore his hair, and rolled up and down on the ground. In a day or two was a love-feast; he stole in, getting behind that none might see him. While Mr. Furze was at prayer, he was seized with a dreadful agony, both of body and mind. This caused many to wrestle with God for him. In a while he sprang up on his feet, stretched out his hands, and cried aloud, "All my sins are forgiven!" At the same instant, one on the other side of the room cried out, "Jesus is mine! And He has taken away all my sins." This was Samuel H. David burst through the people, caught him in his arms, and said, "Come, let us sing the Virgin Mary's song; I never could sing it before. 'My soul doth magnify the Lord, and my spirit doth rejoice in God my Savior.'" And their following behavior plainly showed the reality of their profession.

Smallpox Outbreak

FRIDAY, 23 – I preached at Bath. Riding home we saw a coffin being carried into St. George's church, with many children attending it. When we came near, we found they were our own children, attending a corpse of one of their school fellows, who had died of the smallpox; and God thereby touched many of their hearts in a manner they never knew before.

MONDAY, 26 – I preached to the prisoners in Newgate, and in the afternoon rode over to Kingswood, where I had a solemn watchnight and an opportunity of speaking closely to the children. One is dead, two recovered, seven are ill still; and the hearts of all are like melting wax.

SATURDAY, OCTOBER 1 – I returned to London and found our house in ruins, a great part of it being taken down in order to a thorough repair. But as much remained as I wanted: six foot square suffices me by day or by night.

THURSDAY, DECEMBER 22 – I spent a little time in a visit to Mr. M——; twenty years ago, he was a zealous and useful magistrate, now a picture of human nature in disgrace; feeble in body and mind, slow of speech and of understanding. Lord, let me not live to be useless!

A Desire to Hear

MONDAY, 26 – I was desired to preach at Walsal. James Jones was alarmed at the motion, apprehending there would be much disturbance. However, I determined to make the trial. Coming into the house, I met with a token for good. A woman was telling her neighbor why she came: "I had a desire," said she, "to hear this man; yet I durst not, because I heard so much ill of him; but this morning I dreamed I was praying earnestly, and I heard a voice, saying, 'See the eighth verse of the first chapter of St. John.' I waked and got my Bible, and read, 'He was not that Light, but was sent to bear witness of that Light.' I got up, and came away with all my heart."

Wesley Falls off His Horse

SUNDAY, 8 – I set out for Misterton, though the common road was impassable, being all under water; but we found a way to ride around. I preached at eight, and I saw not one inattentive hearer. In our return, my mare rushing violently through a gate, struck my heel against the gatepost and left me behind her in an instant, laid on my back at full length. She stood still till I rose and mounted again; neither of us was hurt at all.

<hr/>

A Waste of Time

MONDAY, 28 – I spent some hours at the General Assembly, composed of about a hundred and fifty ministers. I was surprised to find 1) that anyone was admitted, even lads, twelve or fourteen years old; 2) that the chief speakers were lawyers, six or seven on one side only; 3) that a single question took up the whole time, which, when I went away, seemed to be as far from a conclusion as ever, namely, "Shall Mr. Lindsay be removed to Kilmarnock parish or not?" The argument for it was, "He has a large family, and this living is twice as good as his own." The argument against it was, "The people are resolved not to hear him and will leave the kirk (church) if he comes. "If then the real point in view had "the greater good of the Church," been, as their law directs, instead of taking up five hours, the debate might have been determined in five minutes.

Love of the Word

About eleven we took horse. While we were dining at Nairn, the innkeeper said, "Sir, the gentlemen of the town have read the little book you gave me on Saturday, and would be glad if you would please to give them a sermon." Upon my consenting, the bell was immediately rung, and the congregation was quickly in the kirk (church). Oh, what a difference is there between South and North Britain! Everyone here at least loves to hear the Word of God, and none takes it into his head to speak one uncivil word to any for endeavoring to save their souls.

Many in Tears

The evening congregation on the hill was by far the largest I have seen in the kingdom, and the most deeply affected. Many were in tears; more seemed cut to the heart. Surely this time will not soon be forgotten. Will it not appear in the annals of eternity?

Where Will You Go?

THURSDAY, 5 – I had the comfort of leaving our brethren at Leeds united in peace and love. About one I preached in a meadow at Wakefield. At first the sun was inconvenient, but it was not many minutes before that inconvenience was removed by the clouds coming between. We had not only a larger, but a far more attentive, congregation than ever was seen here before. One indeed, a kind of gentleman, was walking away with great unconcern when I spoke aloud, "Does Callio care for none of these things? But where will you go, with the wrath of God on your head and the curse of God on your back?" He stopped short, stood still, and went no farther till the sermon was ended.

Moaning Mayor

SUNDAY, 29 – The minister of St. Mary's sent me word he was very willing I should preach in his church; but, before service began, the mayor sent to forbid it; so he preached a very useful sermon himself. The mayor's behavior so disgusted many of the gentry that they resolved to hear where they could; and accordingly flocked together in the evening from all parts of the town. Perhaps the taking up this cross may profit them more than my sermon in the church would have done.

Wesley's Health

MONDAY, 28 – I breakfasted with Mr. Whitefield, who seemed to be an old, old man, being fairly worn out in his Master's service, though he has hardly seen fifty years; and yet it pleases God that I, who am now in my sixty-third year, find no disorder, no weakness, no decay, no difference from what I was at five-and-twenty; only that I have fewer teeth and more grey hairs.

Wesley Falls off his Horse

WEDNESDAY, 18 – Riding through the Borough, all my mare's feet flew up, and she fell with my leg under her. A gentleman, stepping out, lifted me up and helped me into his shop. I was exceedingly sick but was presently relieved by a little hartshorn and water. After resting a few minutes, I took a coach; but when I was cold, found myself much worse, being bruised on my right arm, my breast, my knee, leg, and ankle, which swelled exceedingly.

Speaking Well of Whitefield

1766. FRIDAY, JANUARY 31 – Mr. Whitefield called upon me. He breathes nothing but peace and love. Bigotry cannot stand before him but hides its head wherever he comes.

Grow a Beard

TUESDAY, 29 – In the evening I preached near the preaching-house at Paddiham and strongly insisted on communion with God as the only religion that would avail us. At the close of the sermon came Mr. M. His long, white beard showed that his present disorder was of some continuance. In all other respects, he was quite sensible; but he told me with much concern, "You can have no place in heaven without a beard! Therefore, I beg, let yours grow immediately."

An Accusation of Perfectionism

But that none might imagine I intended a panegyric either on myself or my friends, I guarded against this in the very title page, saying both in the name of myself and them, "Not as though I had already attained, either were already perfect." To the same effect I speak in the conclusion, "These are the same principles and practices of our sect; these are the marks of a true Methodist"; that is, a true Christian, as

I immediately after explain myself: "by these alone do those who are in derision so-called desire to be distinguished from other men."(P. ii.) "By these marks do we labor to distinguish ourselves from those whose minds or lives are not according to the gospel of Christ." (P. 12.)

"Upon this Rusticulus, or Dr. Dodd, says, 'A Methodist, according to Mr. Wesley, is one who is perfect, and sins not in thought, word, or deed.'

"Sir, have me excused. This is not 'according to Mr. Wesley.' I have told all the world I am not perfect; and yet you allow me to be a Methodist. I tell you flatly, I have not attained the character I draw. Will you pin it upon me in spite of my teeth?

"'But Mr. Wesley says, 'the other Methodists have.' I say no such thing. What I say, after having given a scriptural account of a perfect Christian, is this: 'By these marks the Methodists desire to be distinguished from other men; by these we labor to distinguish ourselves.' And do not you yourself desire and labor after the very same thing?

"But you insist, 'Mr. Wesley affirms the Methodists (that is, all Methodists) to be perfectly holy and righteous.' Where do I affirm this? Not in the tract before us. In the front of this I affirm just the contrary; and that I affirm it anywhere else is more than I know. Be pleased, Sir, to point out the place: till this is done, all you add (bitterly enough) is mere brutum fulmen; and the Methodists (so-called) may still declare (without any impeachment of their sincerity) that they do not come to the holy table 'trusting in their own righteousness, but in God's manifold and great mercies.' I am, Sir,

"Yours,
"John Wesley"

Stupid Creatures

Sunday, May 1 – I preached at seven in the new room; in the afternoon at the College kirk (church), in Old Aberdeen. At six, knowing our house could not contain the congregation, I preached in the castle gate, on the paved stones. A large number of people were all attention; but there were many rude, stupid creatures round about them who knew as little of reason as of religion; I never saw such brutes in Scotland before. One of them threw a potato, which fell on my arm; I turned to them, and some were ashamed.

Those who would condemn Wesley for such talk have probably never preached in the open air. Look at Scripture: "One of themselves, even a prophet of their own, said, The Cretians are always liars, evil beasts, slow bellies" (Titus 1:12). —Ray Comfort

Natural Amphitheatre

SUNDAY, 11 – About nine I preached at St. Agnes and again between one and two. At first I took my old stand at Gwennap, in the natural amphitheatre. I suppose no human voice could have commanded such an audience on plain ground; but the ground rising all around gave me such an advantage that I believe all could hear distinctly.

One Silly Man

SUNDAY, 18 – Our room at the Dock contained the morning congregation tolerably well. Between one and two I began preaching on the quay in Plymouth. Notwithstanding the rain, abundance of people stood to hear. But one silly man talked without ceasing, till I desired the people to open to the right and left, and let me look him in the face. They did so. He pulled off his hat and quietly went away.

Time with Whitefield

1769. MONDAY, JANUARY 9 – I spent a comfortable and profitable hour with Mr. Whitefield, in calling to mind the former times and the manner wherein God prepared us for a work which it had not then entered into our hearts to conceive.

More Time with George

MONDAY, 27 (LONDON. 2828 Correct to the text) – I had one more agreeable conversation with my old friend and fellow laborer, George Whitefield. His soul appeared to be vigorous still, but his body was sinking apace; unless God interposes, he must soon finish his labors.

Riding High in April, Shot Down in May

THURSDAY, MAY 25 – I rode to Bandon. In the evening we were obliged to be in the house; but the next, Friday, 26, I stood in the main street, and cried to a numerous congregation, "Fear God and keep his commandments: for this is the whole duty of man" [Ecclesiastes. 12:13). Afterward I visited one that a year or two ago was in high life, an eminent beauty, adored by her husband, admired and caressed by some of the first men in the nation. She was now without husband, without friend, without fortune, confined to her bed, in constant pain, and in black despair, believing herself forsaken of God and possessed by a legion of devils! Yet I found great liberty in praying for her and a strong hope that she will die in peace.

Rotten Eggs

TUESDAY, 19 – Between twelve and one, I preached at Freshford; on White's Hill, near Bradford, in the evening. By this means many had an opportunity of hearing, who would not have come to the room. I had designed to preach there again the next evening, but a gentleman in the town desired me to preach at his door. The beasts of the people were tolerably quiet till I had nearly finished my sermon. They then lifted up their voices, especially one, called a gentleman, who had filled his pocket with rotten eggs. But, a young man coming unawares clapped his hands on each side and mashed them all at once. In an instant he was perfume all over, though it was not so sweet as balsam.

This is wonderful.—Ray Comfort

Full of Himself

SATURDAY, FEBRUARY 3, and at my leisure moments on several of the following days, I read with much expectation a celebrated book—Rousseau upon Education. But how was I disappointed! Sure a more consummate coxcomb never saw the sun! How amazingly full of himself! Whatever he speaks, he pronounces as an oracle. But many of his oracles are as palpably false, as that "young children never love old people." No! Do they never love grandfathers and grandmothers? Frequently more than they do their own parents. Indeed, they love all that love them and that with more warmth and sincerity than when they come to riper years.

But I object to his temper, more than to his judgment: he is a mere misanthrope; a cynic all over. So indeed is his brother-infidel, Voltaire, and well-nigh as great a coxcomb. But he hides both his doggedness and vanity a little better; whereas here it stares us in the face continually.

As to his book, it is whimsical to the last degree, grounded neither upon reason nor experience. To cite particular passages would be endless; but anyone may observe concerning the whole that the advices which are good are trite and common, only disguised under new expressions. And those which are new, which are really his own, are lighter than vanity itself. Such discoveries I always expect from those who are too wise to believe their Bibles.

***

Keep a Loose Rein

WEDNESDAY, 21 – In the following days I went on slowly through Staffordshire and Cheshire to Manchester. In this journey, as well as in many others, I observed a mistake that almost universally prevails; I desire all travelers to take good notice of it, for it may save them both from trouble and danger. Nearly thirty years ago I was thinking, "How is it that no horse ever stumbles while I am reading?" (History, poetry, and philosophy I commonly read on horseback, having other employment at other times.) No account can possibly be given but this: because then I throw the reins on his neck. I then set myself to observe; that in riding above a hundred thousand miles, I scarcely ever remember any horse (except two, that would fall head over heels anyway) to fall or make a considerable stumble while I rode with a slack rein. To fancy, therefore, that a tight rein prevents stumbling is a capital blunder. I have repeated the trial more frequently than most men in the kingdom can do. A slack rein will prevent stumbling if anything will. But in some horses nothing can.

———•·•———

How kind God is to hold a loose reign on us. As Christians, we are called to liberty in Christ. —Ray Comfort

More Stupid Folks

MONDAY, JULY 30 – I preached at Bingham, ten miles from Nottingham. I really admired the exquisite stupidity of the people. They gaped and stared while I was speaking of death and judgment, as if they had never heard of such things before. And they were not helped by two surly, ill-mannered clergymen, who seemed to be just as wise as themselves. The congregation at Houghton in the evening was more noble, behaving with the utmost decency.

TUESDAY, 31 – At nine I preached in the marketplace at Loughborough, to almost as large a congregation as at Nottingham and equally attentive. Thence I rode to Markfield. Notwithstanding the harvest, the church was quickly filled. And great was our rejoicing in our great High Priest, through whom we "came boldly to the throne of grace." In the evening I preached in the Castle Yard at Leicester, to a multitude of awakened and unawakened. One feeble attempt was made to disturb them. A man was sent to cry "fresh salmon" at a little distance; but he might as well have spared the pains, for none took the least notice of him.

Enemies at Peace

TUESDAY, 21 – I rode on to Tiverton, and thence through Launceston, Camelford, Port Isaac, Cubert, St. Agnes, and Redruth, to St. Ives. Here God has made all our enemies to be at peace with us, so that I might have preached in any part of the town. But I rather chose a meadow, where such as would might sit down, either on the grass or on the hedges—so the Cornish term for their broad stone walls, which are usually covered with grass. Here I enforced, "Fear God, and keep his commandments; for this is the whole duty of man."

Twenty Thousand Hear the Gospel

SUNDAY, 2 – At five in the evening I preached in the natural amphitheatre at Gwennap. The people covered a circle of nearly fourscore yards diameter and could not be fewer than twenty thousand. Yet, upon inquiry, I found they could all hear distinctly, it being a calm, still evening.

Wesley Falls off His Horse

FRIDAY, 7, to Taunton. Presently, after preaching, I took horse. The rain obliged us to make haste; but in a while the saddle came over his neck, and then turned under his belly. I had then only to throw myself off, or I would have fallen under him. I was a little bruised, but soon mounted again and rode to Lymphsham, and the next day to Bristol.

Whitefield's Funeral, Wesley's Wife

1771. WEDNESDAY, JANUARY 2 – I preached in the evening, at Deptford, a kind of funeral sermon for Mr. Whitefield. In every place I wish to show all possible respect to the memory of that great and good man.

WEDNESDAY, 23 – For what cause I know not to this day, —[Wesley's wife] set out for Newcastle, purposing "never to return." *Non cam reliqui: non dimisi: non revocabo* [I did not desert her: I did not send her away: I will not recall her.]

Wesley's marriage was a sad part of life.—Ray Comfort

Wesley and Paintings

FRIDAY, FEBRUARY 7 – I called on a friend at Hampton Court, who went with me through the house. It struck me more than anything of the kind I have seen in England, more than Blenheim House itself. One great difference is, everything there appears designedly grand and splendid; here everything is quite, as it were, natural, and one thinks it cannot be otherwise. If the expression may be allowed, there is a kind of stiffness runs through the one, and an easiness through the other. Of pictures I do not pretend to be a judge; but there is one, by Paul Rubens, which particularly struck me, both with the design and the execution of it. It is Zacharias and Elisabeth, with John the Baptist, two or three years old, coming to visit Mary, and our Lord sitting upon her knee. The passions are surprisingly expressed, even in the children; but I could not see either the decency or common sense of painting them stark naked. Nothing can defend or excuse this; it is shockingly absurd, even an Indian being the judge. I allow, a man who paints thus may have a good hand but certainly no brains.

This is one reason I love John Wesley. I am annoyed that the world has statues of king David all over the place, stark naked. Why do they do that? David wore clothes. Why do they insist on painting really ugly pictures of Jesus with plates on His head?—Ray Comfort

From Suicide to the Savior

MONDAY, 17 – One gave me a very remarkable account: A gay young woman lately came up to London. Curiosity led her to hear a sermon, which cut her to the heart. One standing by observed how she was affected and took occasion to talk with her. She lamented that she should hear no more such sermons, as she was to go into the country the next day; but she begged her new acquaintance to write to her there, which she promised to do. In the country her convictions so increased that she resolved to put an end to her own life. With this design she was going upstairs, when her father called her and gave her a letter from London. It was from her new acquaintance, who told her, "Christ is just ready to receive you: now is the day of salvation." She cried out, "It is, it is! Christ is mine!" and was filled with joy unspeakable. She begged her father to give her pen, ink, and paper that she might answer her friend immediately. She told her what God had done for her soul, and added, "We have no time to lose! The Lord is at hand! Now, even now, we are stepping into eternity." She directed her letter, dropped down, and died.

A Cup of Tea

MONDAY, APRIL 6 (MANCHESTER) – In the afternoon I drank tea at Am.O. But how was I shocked! The children that used to cling about me and drink in every word had been at a boarding school. There they had unlearned all religion and even seriousness and had learned pride, vanity, affectation, and whatever could guard them against the knowledge and love of God. Methodist parents who would send your girls headlong to hell, send them to a fashionable boarding school!

Take notice of his words. Avoid sending your children to be educated by a God-hating world. —Ray Comfort

Death, Judgment, Heaven and Hell

WEDNESDAY, 22 – About eight I preached once more in the Masons' Lodge, at Port Glasgow. The house was crowded greatly, and I suppose all the gentry of the town were part of the congregation. Resolving not to shoot over their heads, as I had done the day before, I spoke strongly of death and judgment, heaven and hell. This they seemed to comprehend; and there was no more laughing among them, or talking with each other; but all were quietly and deeply attentive.

Wake Up Ministers

WEDNESDAY, 29 – I went on to Brechin and preached in the town hall to a congregation of all sorts—Seceders, Glassites, Non-jurors, and whatnot. Oh, what excuse have ministers in

Scotland for not declaring the whole counsel of God, where the bulk of the people not only endure, but love plain dealing!

***

Open Air a Cross

SUNDAY, SEPTEMBER 6 – I preached on the quay, at Kingswood, and near King's Square. To this day field-preaching is a cross to me. But I know my commission and see no other way of "preaching the gospel to every creature."

***

Another Angry Mob

MONDAY, 24 – About noon I preached at Tonnylommon. One of my horses having a shoe loose, I borrowed Mr. Watson's horse and left him with the chaise. When we came near Enniskillen, I desired two only to ride with me, and the rest of our friends to keep at a distance. Some masons were at work on the first bridge, who gave us some coarse words. We had abundance more as we rode through the town; but soldiers being in the street and taking knowledge of me in a respectful manner, the mob shrank back. An hour after, Mr. Watson came in the chaise. Before he came to the bridge many ran together and began to throw whatever came next to hand. The bridge itself they had blocked up with large stones so that a carriage could not pass; but an old man cried out, "Is this the way you use strangers?" and rolled away the stones. The mob quickly rewarded him by plastering him over with mortar from head to foot. They then fell upon the carriage, which they cut with stones in several places, and well nigh covered with dirt and mortar. From one end of the town to the other, the stones flew thick about the coachman's head. Some of them were two or three pounds' weight, which they threw with all their might. If but one of them had struck him, it would have effectually prevented him from driving any farther; and, then, doubtless, they would have given an account of the chaise and horses.

I preached at Sydore in the evening and morning, and then set out for Roosky. The road lay not far from Enniskillen. When we came pretty near the town, both men and women saluted us, first with bad words and then with dirt and stones. My horses soon left them behind, but not till they had broken one of the windows, the glass of which came pouring in upon me; but did me no further hurt.

About an hour after, John Smith came to Enniskillen. The masons on the bridge preparing for battle, he was afraid his horse would leap with him into the river; and therefore chose to alight. Immediately they poured in upon him a whole shower of dirt and stones. However, he made his way through the town, though pretty much daubed and bruised.

WEDNESDAY, 26 – We set out at half-hour past two, and reached Omagh a little before eleven. Finding I could not reach Ding Bridge by two o'clock in the chaise, I rode forward with all the speed I could; but the horse dropping a shoe, I was so retarded that I did not reach the place till between three and four. I found the minister and the people waiting; but the church would not nearly contain them, so I preached near it to a mixed multitude of rich and poor, churchmen, Papists, and Presbyterians. I was a little weary and faint when I came, the sun having shone exceedingly hot; but the number and behavior of the congregation made me forget my own weariness.

Having a good horse, I rode to the place where I was to lodge (two miles off) in about an hour. After tea they told me another congregation was waiting, so I began preaching without delay. I warned them of the madness which was spreading among them, namely, leaving the church. Most of them, I believe, will take the advice; I hope all that are of our society.

Over Thirty Thousand

SATURDAY, 21 – I preached in Illogan and at Redruth; Sunday, 22, in St. Agnes church town, at eight; about one at Redruth; and at five, in the amphitheatre at Gwennap. The people both filled it and covered the ground round about to a considerable distance. Supposing the space to be fourscore yards square and to contain five persons in a square yard, there must be above two and thirty thousand people, the largest assembly I ever preached to. Yet I found, upon inquiry, all could hear even to the skirts of the congregation! Perhaps the first time that a man of seventy had been heard by thirty thousand persons at once!

The Same Strength

TUESDAY, 28 – This being my birthday, the first day of my seventy-second year, I was considering how is it that I find just the same strength as I did thirty years ago? That my sight is considerably better now and my nerves firmer than they were then? That I have none of the infirmities of old age and have lost several I had in my youth? The grand cause is the good pleasure of God who doeth whatsoever pleaseth Him. The chief means are: 1) my constantly rising at four, for about fifty years; 2) my generally preaching at five in the morning, one of the most healthy exercises in the world; 3) my never traveling less, by sea or land, than four thousand five hundred miles in a year.

Drinking in the Word

TUESDAY, APRIL 30 – in the evening I preached in a kind of square at Colne, to a multitude of people, all drinking in the Word. I scarcely ever saw a congregation wherein men, women, and children stood in such a posture; and this in the town wherein, thirty years ago, no Methodist could show his head! The first that preached here was John Jane, who was innocently riding through the town when the zealous mob pulled him off his horse and put him in the stocks. He seized the opportunity and vehemently exhorted them "to flee from the wrath to come."

Wesley Falls off his Horse

I set out for Douglas in the one-horse chaise, Mrs. Smyth riding with me. In about an hour, in spite of all I could do, the headstrong horse ran the wheel against a large stone and the chaise overset in a moment. But we fell so gently on smooth grass that neither of us was hurt at all. In the evening I preached at Douglas to nearly as large a congregation as that at Peel, but not nearly so serious. Before ten we went on board and about twelve on Tuesday, 3, landed at Whitehaven. I preached at five in the afternoon; hastening to Cockermouth, I found a large congregation waiting in the castle yard. Between nine and ten o'clock I took chaise, and about ten on Wednesday, 4, reached Settle. In the evening I preached near the market place, and all but two or three gentlefolks were seriously attentive. Thursday, 5. About noon I came to Otley.

***

Some Bad Words

MONDAY, JULY 21 – Having been much pressed to preach at Jatterson, a colliery six or seven miles from Pembroke, I began soon after seven. The house was presently filled and all the space about the doors and windows; the poor people drank in every word. I had finished my sermon when a gentleman, violently pressing in, bade the people get home and mind their business. As he used some bad words, my driver spoke to him. He fiercely said, "Do you think I need to be taught by a chaise-boy?" The lad replying, "Really, sir, I do think so," the conversation ended.

Could Not Improve

TUESDAY, SEPTEMBER 1 – I went to Tiverton. I was musing here on what I heard a good man say long since—"Once in seven years I burn all my sermons; for it is a shame if I cannot write better sermons now than I could seven years ago." Whatever others can do, I really cannot. I cannot write a better sermon on the Good Steward than I did seven years ago; I cannot write a better on the Great Assize than I did twenty years ago; I cannot write a better on the Use of Money, than I did nearly thirty years ago; nay, I know not that I can write a better on the Circumcision of the Heart than I did five-and-forty years ago. Perhaps, indeed, I may have read five or six hundred books more than I had then, and may know a little more history, or natural philosophy, than I did; but I am not sensible that this has made any essential addition to my knowledge in divinity. Forty years ago I knew and preached every Christian doctrine which I preach now.

The Fear of God

SUNDAY, 29 – I was desired to preach a charity sermon in St. Luke's church, Old Street. I doubt whether it was ever so crowded before; the fear of God seemed to possess the whole audience. In the afternoon I preached at the new chapel; and at seven, in St. Margaret's, Rood Lane, fully as much crowded as St. Luke's. Is then the scandal of the cross ceased?

The fear of God is missing in today's pews because it is missing in today's pulpits. Sinners will never depart from sin when they don't fear God.—Ray Comfort

Seized by the Wife

MONDAY, 12 – About eleven, I preached at Newton-upon-Trent, to a large and very genteel congregation. Thence we went to Newark, but our friends were divided as to the place where I should preach. At length they found a convenient place, covered on three sides and on the fourth open to the street. It contained two or three thousand people well, who appeared to hear as for life. Only one big man, exceedingly drunk, was very noisy and turbulent till his wife seized him by the collar, gave him two or three hearty boxes on the ear, and dragged him away like a calf. But at length he got out of her hands, crept in among the people, and stood as quiet as a lamb.

It's a pity that more wives don't do this when their husbands are given to alcohol. A strong reproof may have been the reason he came back to listen.—Ray Comfort

Condemned Criminals

SUNDAY, DECEMBER 26 – I preached the condemned criminals sermon in Newgate. Forty-seven were under sentence of death. While they were coming in, there was something very awful in the clink of their chains. But no sound was heard, either from them or the crowded audience, after the text was named: "There is joy in heaven over one sinner that repents, more than over ninety and nine just persons, that need not repentance" [see Luke 15:7]. The power of the Lord was eminently present, and most of the prisoners were in tears. A few days after, twenty of them died at once, five of whom died in peace. I could not but greatly approve of the spirit and behavior of Mr. Villette, the ordinary; and I rejoiced to hear that it was the same on all similar occasions.

Nothing Wrong

1786. MONDAY, JANUARY 9 – At leisure hours this week I read the Life of Sir William Penn, a wise and good man. But I was much surprised at what he relates concerning his first wife who lived, I suppose, fifty years and said a little before her death, "I bless God, I never did anything wrong in my life!" Was she then ever convinced of sin? And if not, could she be saved on any other tooting than a heathen?

Necessity Was Laid Upon Me

APRIL, 12 (DUBLIN) – (BEING EASTER DAY) We had a solemn assembly indeed; many hundred communicants in the morning, and in the afternoon far more hearers than our room would contain, though it is now considerably enlarged. Afterward I met the society and explained to them at large the original design of the Methodists, namely, not to be a distinct party but to stir up all parties, Christians or heathens, to worship God in spirit and in truth; but the Church of England in particular, to which they belonged from the beginning. With this view I have uniformly gone on for fifty years, never varying from the doctrine of the Church at all; nor from her discipline, of choice, but of necessity; so, in a course of years, necessity was laid upon me (as I have proved elsewhere) 1) to preach in the open air; 2) to pray extempore; 3) to form societies; 4) to accept of the assistance of lay preachers; and, in a few other instances, to use such means as occurred, to prevent or remove evils that we either felt or feared.

The Greek word for "necessity" means "a continual, intense distress." —Ray Comfort

---

Don't miss these other helpful publications:

The Way of the Master (Bridge-Logos)

Hell's Best Kept Secret (Whitaker House)

Spurgeon Gold (Bridge-Logos)

Whitefield Gold (Bridge-Logos)

The World's Greatest Preachers (Whitaker House)

The School of Biblical Evangelism textbook (Bridge-Logos Publishers)

How to Win Souls and Influence People (Bridge-Logos)

God Doesn't Believe in Atheists (Bridge-Logos)

Out of the Comfort Zone (Bridge-Logos)

A Full House of Growing Pains (Bridge-Logos)

Hollywood Be Thy Name (Bridge-Logos)

What Did Jesus Do? (Genesis Publishing Group)

The Way of the Master for Kids (Genesis Publishing Group)

Behind the Scenes: The Way of the Master (Genesis Publishing Group)

The Way of the Master Minute: A Devotional for Busy Christians (Bridge-Logos)

How to Live Forever … Without Being Religious (Bridge-Logos)

The Evidence Bible (Bridge-Logos)

Listen to The Way of the Master Radio daily.
See www.WayoftheMaster.com

The Way of the Master
P.O. Box 1172 • Bellflower, CA 90706

More **Bridge-Logos** Titles
from Ray Comfort

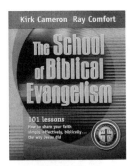

The School of Biblical Evangelism

In this comprehensive study course, you will learn how to share our faith simply, effectively, and biblically … the way Jesus did. Discover the God-given evangelistic tools that will enable you to confidently talk about the Savior.

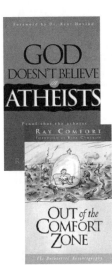

Pure Gold Classics

AN EXPANDING COLLECTION OF THE BEST-LOVED CHRISTIAN CLASSICS OF ALL TIME.

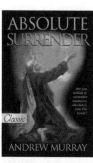

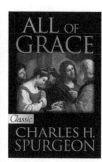

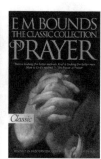

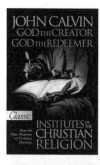

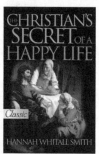

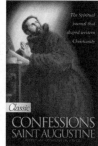

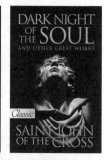

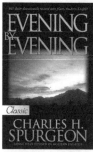

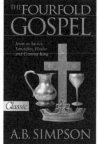

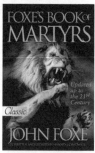

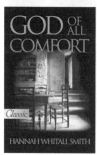

SENSITIVELY REVISED IN MODERN ENGLISH

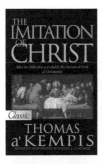

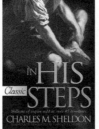

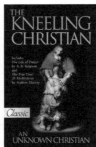

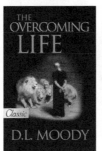

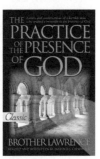

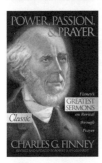

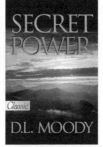

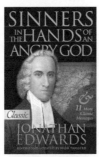

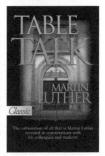

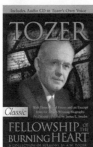

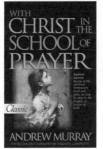

AVAILABLE AT FINE CHRISTIAN BOOKSTORES